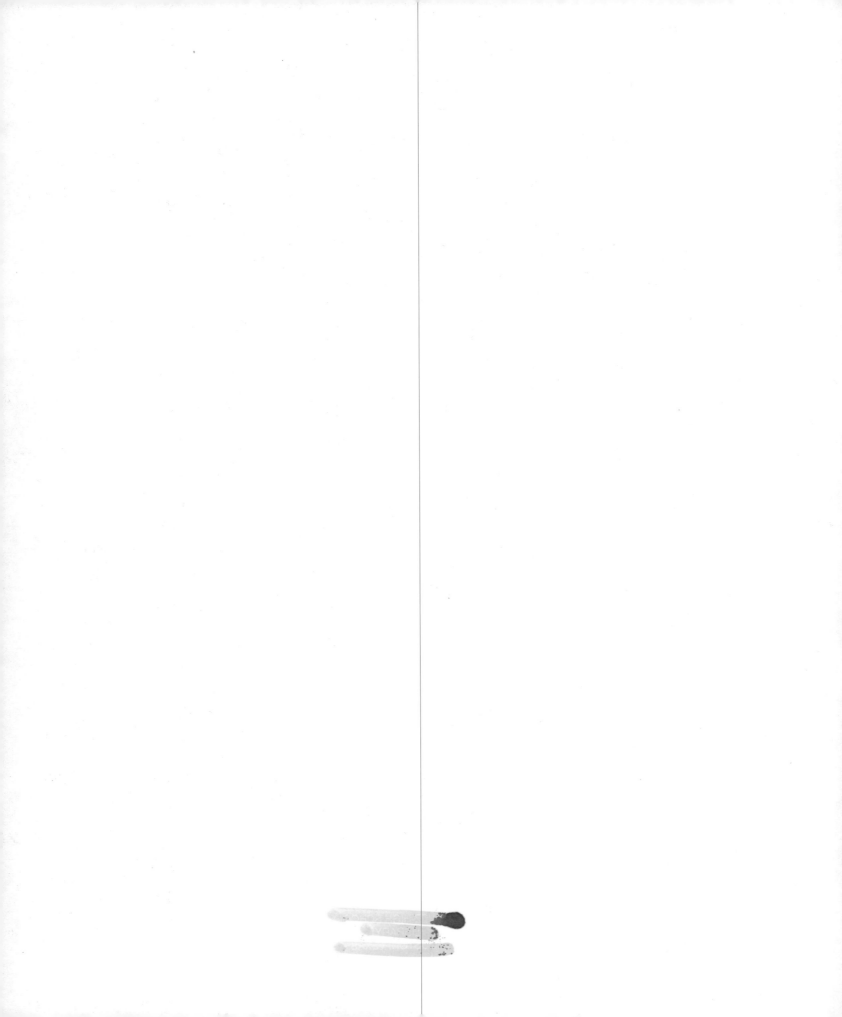

—— THE ——
UNEXPLAINED

MAKING
CONTACT

Produced by Carlton Books Limited
20 Mortimer Street
London, W1N 7RD

First published in hardback edition in 2001 by Chelsea House Publishers, a subsidiary of Haights Cross Communications. Printed and bound in Dubai.

First Printing
1 3 5 7 9 8 6 4 2

The Chelsea House World Wide Web address is http://www.chelseahouse.com

Library of Congress Cataloging-in-Publication Data applied for

Historic Realms of Marvels and Miracles ISBN: 0-7910-6076-4
Ancient Worlds, Ancient Mysteries ISBN: 0-7910-6077-2
Lost Worlds and Forgotten Secrets ISBN: 0-7910-6078-0
We Are Not Alone ISBN: 0-7910-6079-9
Imagining Other Worlds ISBN: 0-7910-6080-2
Coming from the Skies ISBN: 0-7910-6081-0
Making Contact ISBN: 0-7910-6082-9

THE UNEXPLAINED

MAKING CONTACT

Alien Affairs

Hilary Evans

Chelsea House Publishers

Philadelphia

THE
UNEXPLAINED

MAKING
CONTACT

Historic Realms of Marvels and Miracles

Ancient Worlds, Ancient Mysteries

Lost Worlds and Forgotten Secrets

We Are Not Alone

Imagining Other Worlds

Coming From the Skies

CONTENTS

MAKING CONTACT

"Since 1952, Mr Adamski has repeatedly claimed contacts with spacemen. He has claimed to have ridden in their spaceships, on trips round Venus and the moon. He has published photographs alleged to be pictures of UFO scouts and mother-ships. These reports and pictures have been called fakes by several critics. But Adamski's believers insist he is an honest, persecuted man."

When people first reported seeing Flying Saucers in 1947, their stories were widely accepted; when people later reported seeing their occupants, they too were generally able to obtain a sympathetic hearing. But when individuals started claiming that they had *met* the occupants, they came up against a barrier of skepticism. Major Donald Keyhoe, writing in the newsletter of his organization NICAP – the National Investigations Committee on Aerial Phenomena – recognized the importance of settling the matter:

> False or true, the sensational nature of his claims has kept many people from seriously considering the verified UFO evidence. For this reason, it is vitally important that Adamski's stories either be proved beyond question – or, if false, that they be completely discredited.

Yet, logically, it was inevitable that closer contact would take place sooner or later. If the flying saucers were space ships, they must have had occupants, and distant observations would surely lead to closer encounters. What provoked skepticism was partly the stories themselves, and partly those who told them. The stories were so far-fetched that they would hardly have been believed even if told by the most believable people, and those who told them were simply not the most believable people.

No two contact stories are exactly alike, but they run to a fairly predictable pattern. Typically, they comprise a series of episodes:

- The contactee often has premonitions that something special is in store – at least, so we are told after the event.

Jodie Foster and Matthew McConaughey in the 1997 film Contact.

- Even if the contactee is surprised by the contact when it comes, the surprise doesn't last long. He or she rapidly adjusts to the circumstances and is soon on good terms with the aliens. These are generally more or less human in appearance, communicate easily enough either in the contactee's own tongue or by telepathy, and are friendly and well-intentioned.
- Generally, they invite him or her aboard their vessel and give a guided tour of the craft. Often they treat the contactee to a journey in space, though instead of allowing their guest to enjoy the sights, they tend to deliver a lecture comparing Earth with other civilizations. The comparison is invariably to Earth's disadvantage.
- After returning to Earth, life for a contactee will never be the same again. For some, there will be just the one experience, while for others there will be further encounters. But almost always there is a message, to be passed on to the rest of mankind. Usually it contains a warning of what dreadful things will happen if Earthpeople go on being so materialist and aggressive. Sometimes a contactee will be given "official" status as the visitors' representative on Earth.
- For a while, the contactee is likely to enjoy a period of notoriety, during

A spacecraft looms over the car of humans who have been lined up for abduction.

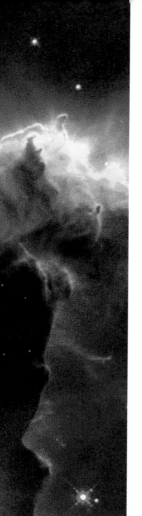

which he or she is a guest on radio chat shows, gives lectures, stars at flying saucer conventions, and publishes (often with the help of a ghost writer) an account of the adventure. Sometimes he or she becomes the centre of a cult or the founder of a School of spiritual enlightenment, or may diversify into ecology, free energy machine design, radical politics, or some other New Age activity.

THE CONTACTEES

The contactees are a varied crowd. Consider a handful of them:

George Adamski was brought by his parents to the United States from Poland at age two. He claimed to have been educated privately, by extraterrestrials, at "the highest school of Cosmic Law at a monastery in Tibet"; after six years study he graduated, styled himself "Professor", and founded the occult-mystico-philosophical "Royal Order of Tibet"

Orfeo Angelucci's leisure-time interest was scientific experiment so he was not surprised to be contacted by extraterrestrials.

in order to pass his knowledge on to others. During Prohibition, he used the Order as a cover for trading in bootleg liquor: at the time of his encounter, he was working in a friend's restaurant on Mount Palomar, California.

Orfeo Angelucci was a sickly child who spent much of his early years in hospital for "organic weakness". He authored a thesis on The Nature of Infinite Entities which he mailed to eminent scientists, but none of them showed interest. At the time of his encounter, he was working at the Lockheed plant in California. In his leisure time, he conducted "scientific experiments" – it was when he sent up materials in balloons that he attracted the attention of a flying saucer which happened to be close by.

Rose C was described by science-fiction writer Jimmy Guieu as "an average Frenchwoman". At the time of her encounter she was 24, divorced with a 4-year old child, living with her widowed father in southern France.

Stefan Denaerde was a well-to-do Dutch businessman, living in Den Haag.

Truman Bethurum was a construction engineer, working in the desert.

Woodrow Derenberger was the manager of an appliance store in West Virginia.

Aladino Felix – a.k.a. "Dino Kraspedon" – was a former theological student, well educated, living in Sao Paulo, Brazil with his wife and children.

Daniel Fry, though described on the wrapper of his book as "the best informed scientist in the world on the subject of space and space travel", was an obscure engineer whose achievements were limited to minor developments in missile systems. His Ph.D. was purchased from an English institution in exchange for a 10,000 word thesis and a cash payment.

George King had been concerned with esoteric matters from an early age, so was mentally prepared for his experiences: "When I was fifteen, I knew that one day I would visit other worlds." He practised yoga for ten years before his contact, and was a faith healer. A colleague reported that "he had successfully and repeatedly demonstrated all psychic powers then commonly known," though it is not stated when, where or to whom he demonstrated them. In May 1954, he heard a voice telling him "Prepare

yourself! You are to become the voice of Interplanetary Parliament." A few days later, "an Indian Swami of world renown" unexpectedly materialized in his apartment.

Eduard "Billy" Meier saw his first UFO at age 5, and began receiving telepathic communications shortly after. During the 1960s, he found his way to an ashram in India, where he met Asket, from the DAL Universe. Later he settled in his native Switzerland.

Frenchman **Pierre Monnet** recalled that, at kindergarten during break, he sat on a bench and thought deeply about the immensity of the universe. "I looked up at the skies and thought "What are the other me's doing on other worlds? Are they playing games, or are they, too, thinking?"... That a child of four should think like that may seem to you impossible, but I assure you I'm not making it up."

CONTACT

This mixed bag of individuals all share one thing in common: they all believed they had met extraterrestrials. Most of them also believed they had been specially chosen for the privilege after being watched by the aliens, sometimes since infancy. Howard Menger, in 1932 – when he was ten – had a meeting with "the most exquisite woman my young eyes had ever beheld" who told him "I have come a long way to see you, Howard, and to talk with you". Her people – she is a Venusian – had been observing him for a long time and now, she told him, "We are contacting our own". Though from Saturn, at the time of his later experiences he was working as a sign painter. His wife Connie/Marla, who was born on Venus, says

> I had been mentally space traveling since I was a child. I can remember the tingling sensation when I looked up at the stars ... longing, waiting for some ephemeral [sic] lover.

Her mother used to take her to

French contactee "Rose C." was an ordinary person with an everyday lifestyle who had a brief encounter with aliens, then relapsed again into obscurity.

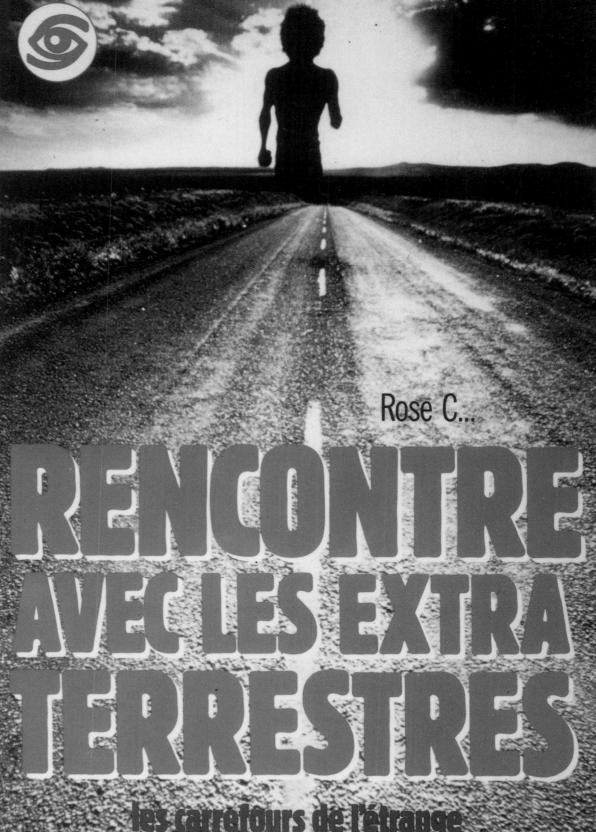

Rose C...

RENCONTRE AVEC LES EXTRA TERRESTRES

les carrefours de l'étrange
EDITIONS DU ROCHER

Pierre Monnet had speculated about other worlds since early childhood: this photo was taken three years after his contact with aliens.

lectures in New York, "usually on metaphysics and allied subjects". While married to her first, terrestrial husband, she had "a strange feeling that I was being observed – that someone was watching, waiting …"

In June 1946, Menger again met the Venusian lady of his boyhood encounter. She revealed that despite her appearance, she was more than 500 years old. This was followed by frequent meetings with aliens from Venus, Mars and elsewhere:

> The nature of the meetings required that many of them take place at night. Often I would receive such mental impressions between 1:00 and 2:00am, and, while my wife lay sleeping, I would drive away to meet the space people and be given further instructions pertaining to my work.

This work largely consisted of helping the aliens adjust to earth conditions:

he cut their hair, and one day was instructed to buy several outfits of female clothing.

> The women went into the next room, from which I soon heard a series of giggles and groans. Finally the door opened and the bras were flung out. They apologized, saying they just could not wear them, and they never had. Just why I didn't know, and you may be certain that I felt it wise not to ask!

On July 4, 1950, Daniel Fry discovered that it was a warm evening and his air conditioner was malfunctioning, so he took a walk in the neighbourhood of his place of work, White Sands Proving Ground. About 9pm, he saw a strange shaped object descend to ground level; he walked towards it to investigate, and found himself close to what was evidently an alien spacecraft. He was about to touch it when a voice warned "Better not touch the hull, pal, it's still hot!" Taken by surprise, he stumbled back, tripped and fell, at which the voice added "Take it easy, pal, you're among friends."

The speaker, A-lan, was actually more than 1300 km away, observing him from a mother craft. He invited Fry to enter the ship which, though a cargo carrier, was conveniently furnished with four earth-style seats. A-lan explained he was from a civilization which had more or less made itself independent of planetary life, and permanently inhabited huge artificial spacecraft.

In July 1951, 19-year old Pierre Monnet had been visiting his fiancée who lived in a village a few kilometres away. He was cycling home to his house in Orange in south-east France, when he and his bicycle were suddenly teleported to a quarry some 5 km the far side of the town. He dismounted at the entrance to the quarry, made his way into it "as if directed by an irresistible force". There he saw a domed disc some 15–20 metres in diameter hovering over the ground, giving off a blue-white glow which lit up the surroundings. As he got closer, the sounds of everyday life seemed to fade away.

Four "human beings" wearing close-fitting clothes were standing near the disc. They were beautiful, seemingly sexless, with long, neatly combed blond

hair. Their look radiated gentleness, goodness and peacefulness. They imprinted a long message on his memory, which he was later able to transcribe perfectly. They also – though he wasn't aware of it at the time – took him on board their spaceship to perform an operation of "regeneration", which enabled him to live to the age of 120.

He turned away without saying goodbye, and remounted his bike. Then it seems he must have been teleported again, for the next thing he knew, he was arriving at the outskirts of Orange at the same time he had left his girlfriend's village, 1.30 am.

On March 23, 1952 – his thirty-third birthday – Sicilian Eugenio Siragusa was waiting at a bus-stop to go to work, as a customs official, when he saw a strange object in the sky. This was followed by telepathic communications instructing him in his role as "Messenger". Ten years later, on October 30, 1962, he received a sudden impulse to go up onto nearby Mount Etna. He had the feeling that he was not driving the car, but that it was controlled by a superior force. Once at his destination, he met two beings in spaceman-like costume who gave him a message before returning to their disc.

On May 3, 1952, Orfeo Angelucci felt odd while working at the Lockheed plant. Driving home, he saw a strange disc-shaped object in the sky; thinking it "one of those flying saucers I had read about", he pulled off the highway to observe it. Two smaller objects separated from the disc, descended and hovered near his car. A voice told him, in perfect English, not to be afraid. The entity – still unseen – informed him they had been observing him ever since his balloon experiment. He was the most important of three who had been chosen for contact; another lived in Rome, a third in India.

He was given information about flying saucers and the visitors' mission: "With deep compassion and understanding we have watched your world going through its "growing pains". We ask that you look upon us simply as older brothers; we will aid Earth's people insofar as they, through free will, will permit us to do so." They then said that they would contact him again.

On July 27–28, 1952, Truman

Bethurum was out in the Nevada desert in his truck. He had been taking "a little snooze" in its cabin, and he woke around midnight to find himself surrounded by small, strange-looking uniformed men. He began conversing with them, then saw the Saucer hovering nearby. He was taken to its Captain, who turned out to be a very attractive and friendly lady named Aura Rhanes. She invited him to sit down, and they talked for quite a while.

On November 20, 1952, George Adamski and a group of friends drove out into the desert, hoping to see saucers. At Desert Center, after seeing a "mother ship", he asked a friend to drive him away from the others and leave him alone. He then met a Venusian from a small flying saucer; they talked for some time, chiefly by telepathy. The Venusian left footprints in the sand with enigmatic markings: one of his companions, ancient astronaut theorist George Hunt Williamson, had thoughtfully brought along some plaster of paris, so able to take a mould. His companions, though at a distance of a km or more, later signed sworn affidavits that they witnessed the encounter.

Buck Nelson, an Ozark farmer, saw his first flying saucer on July 30, 1954. It shot a ray at him which permanently cured his lumbago and neuritis. On February 1, 1955, a saucer hovered over his farm, and a voice called down to ask if he was friendly. He replied that he was. On March 5, he was again visited by the Saucer. This time it landed, and three aliens emerged, one of them an Earthman who has been living on Venus for the previous couple of years. They had their dog with them. They stopped by and chatted for an hour or so until it was time to be getting along, but they promised to return.

One day in May 1957, sisters Helen and Betty Mitchell stopped off for a coke in a downtown St Louis coffee shop where they met Elen and Zelas, crewmen from a huge mother-craft that was orbiting Earth. Their visitors told them the Space People had been watching them for the past eight years, and indeed had been noting their progress since birth. The sisters suspected a leg-pull, but at a second meeting they were shown how to construct a simple device which enabled them to communicate with the Space People.

In July 1967, Stefan Denaerde was sailing with his family in the Oosterscheldt, on the Dutch coast, when his boat hit a submerged object. While investigating the cause, he rescued a body, which turned out to be that of an alien being. The submerged object was in fact an alien spacecraft. In return for rescuing their colleague, the occupants invited him aboard their craft. He was treated to an 8-hour instruction session, while his family remained in the boat nearby. Initially they conversed in English, but subsequently used a form of universal pre-Babel language which seemed to him to be Dutch, but was in fact "the language of all living species in this universe: even a plant or an animal will understand it". They gave a detailed account of life on their planet, Iarga, which is largely covered with water; the population density is 6000/ km^2 – 18 times as high as that of the densely populated Netherlands! This did present problems, but the Iargans resolved them with admirable ingenuity.

On August 11, 1969, Frenchman Jean Miguères was driving his ambulance, carrying a patient – who in fact had died during the trip – from Perpignan to Rouen. Nearing the end of his journey,

The aliens preferred to make contacts in out-of-the-way locations: no one beside engineer Truman Bethurum saw this huge "scow" when it landed in the Nevada desert.

Unlike today's abductors, the aliens encountered by the contactees were mostly of the type classified as "Blond Nordic", human-like and often indistinguishable from Earth people.

feel any pain and won't suffer at all as a result of this accident. From now on, you will be much stronger than before. I am going to "regenerate" you by a process not yet known on your planet.

Miguères later learned that the whole event had been monitored by the extraterrestrials.

We did not provoke anything, Earthman, all we did was orchestrate an event which was going to happen in any case ... Thanks to our detector, we saw the crazy car long before you did ... a rapid inquiry to our computer, whose sophistication is beyond your knowledge, told us the accident could not be avoided ... thanks to a magnetic field of a power surpassing your imagination, we were able to control the danger of fire and thus save the lives of the occupants of your vehicle.

"In fact, then, you were using me as a sort of guinea-pig?" Miguères asked. "Yes, in a way," the alien admitted, but then reminded him that without their intervention he would have been killed ...

During April 1975, John H Womack was driving down a lonely country road in the Tennessee Valley, North Alabama, when a ball of fire dropped through the sky onto the road. While he was watching it, a 50-metre disc appeared and hovered over a nearby meadow, humming gently. A beam of light deprived him of consciousness: the next thing he knew, he was sitting inside the vessel with a helmet on his head in a room full of gadgetry, surrounded by a variety of non-human entities. By means of a box connected to his helmet, the leader explained their good intentions, and gave Womack information about them.

Womack was surprised by how happy and relaxed he felt; the extraterrestrial explained that this was thanks to a pill he had just swallowed, an "anti-demon pill".

You are experiencing life completely free of demons for the first time. Demons exist throughout the universe. Demons are real, not just states of mind as most people

Helen and Betty Mitchell, two contactees from St Louis, tell of their exciting meeting with two handsome Space Brothers.

at 5.30am, he experienced unfamiliar physical sensations, and "felt" that someone was speaking to him, saying:

Don't be afraid – let yourself be guided, no harm will come to you, we are here to protect you and it will all be like a story for you, you will feel nothing, we order you to be calm ...

He noticed a strange cloud head of him, hovering over the road halfway between his ambulance and an approaching car. The dials on his dashboard immediately went haywire.

The approaching car was in the middle of the road, but when Miguères tried to avoid it, it seemed to direct itself at him, and there was no way he could avoid a collision. He was travelling at 140 km/h, the other vehicle at 160 km/h, and the accident was appalling. The other driver was killed, and he himself was trapped inside the wreckage and very badly injured. It seemed to him as though a being materialized in the seat beside him, and said (in French):

Don't worry, you only seem to be injured; in reality, you're not hurt at all. You won't

WE MET THE SPACE PEOPLE

THE STORY OF THE MITCHELL SISTERS
BY HELEN and BETTY MITCHELL

$1.00

SAUCERIAN PUBLICATIONS, CLARKSBURG, W.VA.

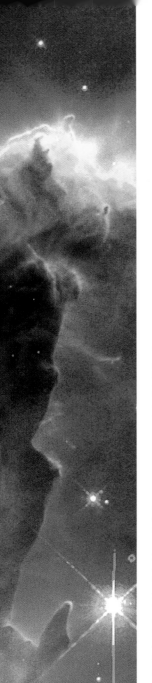

think. They are not visible to the eye, but they do exist on a higher plane of living. Demons are able to invade our minds and cause us to be evil, greedy, selfish, and unhappy. The pill I gave you has driven all demons and their influences from your mind, leaving you with nothing but pure joy in your soul. The anti-demon pill is our greatest discovery. It eliminates all forms of hate, jealousy, greed, misery and wars. It causes a person to be completely happy with just being alive. A person who is demon-free has no need for material possessions to give him a false feeling of security. When the mind is free of demons, only love and joy is left inside …

Womack saw much more, including a video of life on the aliens' (unidentified) planet; then he was returned to where he left his car. Regrettably, he did not think to bring a packet of those Anti-Demon Pills back with him.

THE ENTITIES

As a rule, the beings encountered by contactees are more or less humanoid, but with slight distinctive differences. All adjust without much difficulty to Earth's atmosphere, though Rose C's visitors found it exhausting, and Schmidt's contact took three cautious breaths before removing her mask. Derenberger's Indrid Cold from Lanulos was entirely human in appearance and behaviour; the pair of them communicated telepathically. Many of the visitors can, and often do,

George Adamski's meeting with Orthon from Venus, witnessed by his companions at a distance, may qualify as the first recorded alien encounter.

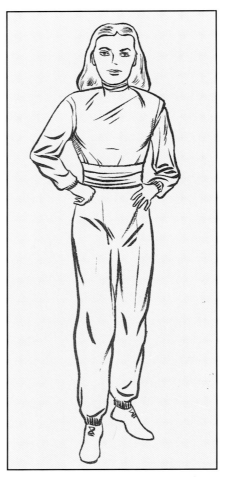

Orthon found no difficulty in adapting to Earth temperature, atmosphere and gravity, though our conditions differ vastly from his home planet, Venus.

pass for human when circumstances require: Brazilian Aladino Felix's visitors were so human-like that his wife took one to be a visiting priest.

Adamski's Venusian, Orthon, was entirely human in appearance, except that "the beauty of his form surpassed anything I had ever seen" and "from him was radiating a feeling of infinite understanding and kindness". The sketch by Alice Wells, made while watching the interview through binoculars, showed a figure of indeterminate sex. Adamski commented that it fell far short of doing justice to the Venusian.

Angelucci didn't see his Luciferan entities during his first contact, but they spoke to him in perfect English. When he met "Neptune", the being was totally human in appearance, "but just to be in his presence was to sense a tremendous uplifting wave of strength, harmony, joy and serenity". When he subsequently met the "dazzlingly beautiful" Lyra,

Angelucci's response was more of the earth, earthy – this was reflected for all to see as "an ugly mottled red and black cloud" in his aura, to the embarrassment of all present. Later, though, he was privileged to enjoy a more spiritual form of relationship with her.

Bethurum's people from Clarion were small humanoids, not much over 1.5 metres tall. Despite her small stature, he described Aura Rhanes, the captain of the alien spacecraft, as a "queen of women": she wore a black velvet bodice with red ribbons and matching beret. Denaerde's Iargans were basically human, but with dog-like faces and grey skin. In view of the cramped living conditions on Iarga, it was just as well they were shorter and more compact than humans. The greatest difference between them and us however was that they "think collectively", rather than as individuals.

George King, probably the most intelligent of all the contactees, was exceptional also in that his contacts were mostly with disembodied beings more evolved than ourselves and existing on a higher plane of existence. However, in the course of his 1956 Mars escapade, he travelled in a space ship whose Venusian operator:

> looked like an incandescent egg suspended about a foot from the floor, for he had discarded his physical body as soon as the action began. His physical body, in a state of semi-dematerialization, looked like a little grey cloud. It was fastened in a locker by a system of magnets.

Communication was extra-sensory. Language, indeed, seems never to be a problem. Often, of course, communication is telepathic, but when actual speech is involved, the aliens have generally acquired the language of the contactee in advance, though they are apt to speak it in a somewhat stilted fashion. Adamski and Orthon communicated by sign and telepathy at their first encounter, but by their next meeting the clever Venusian had mastered English.

Siragusa's "Cosmic Brothers" spoke to him in Italian, Vorilhon's humanoid contacts spoke French perfectly: Felix's spoke fluent Portuguese, and Elizabeth Klarer's lover spoke perfect English.

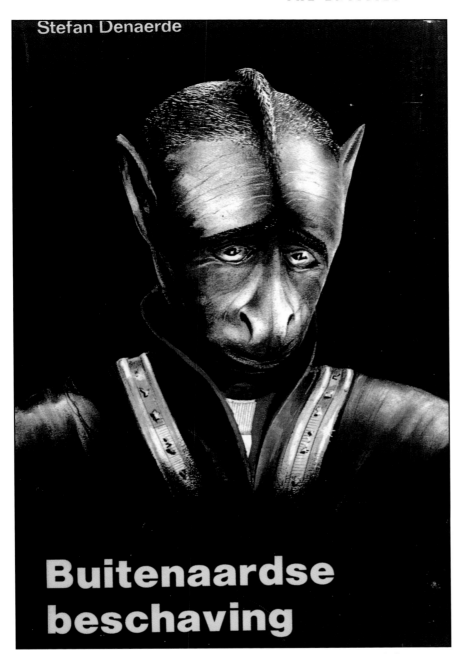

Stefan Denaerde

Buitenaardse beschaving

Though human-like in all other respects, the largans encountered by Dutch businessman Stefan Denaerde had dog-like faces and thought collectively rather than as individuals.

One of Bethurum's companions told him "We have no difficulty with any language", but they showed themselves to be more at home with English than in their French, which was only schoolboy level. German-speaking Reinhold Schmidt said of his Saturnians that "any one of them could have walked unnoticed among our people". However, they spoke English with a German accent, and among themselves they talked in German – that is, when they talked at all: mostly they communicated by telepathy.

THE SPACECRAFT

Since most contactees enter their visitor's spacecraft, and the majority take flights in them, it goes without saying that the craft are "nuts-and-bolts" structures made on a human scale. There are no reports of craft of either Lilliputian or Brobdingnagian proportions, with the exception of George King who described "mother ships" over 800 kilometres long.

Virtually every alien spacecraft which enters Earth's atmosphere is disc-shaped – often, though, these are no more than scouts, associated with an interstellar "mother ship" which does not enter the atmosphere. Dan Martin, for example, was levitated into a scout ship which ferried him to a larger interplanetary craft, equipped much like an ocean liner here on Earth.

No two space ships are exactly alike, but this is only to be expected since it is rare for two sets of visitors to come from the same place of origin. Rose C's visitors' vessel was "shaped like one of Maurice Chevalier's hats" but was the size of a bus. Menger's spacecraft were saucer, disc, bell and other shapes – their appearance could vary according to the magnetic fields surrounding them. In the atmosphere, they could "travel in excess of 32,000 kilometres per hour; outside the earth's atmosphere, they can exceed the speed of light".

Most witnesses display a natural curiosity about the technology of the craft, and generally their hosts are happy to show off their vessels – often in tedious detail. It is noteworthy that the equipment is invariably designed with the expectation that the user will have hands to pull handles and fingers to push buttons. All have a force of gravity, whether natural or artificial, and such factors as temperature, air pressure, humidity and so on are at levels similar to Earth. No contactee has ever complained of being too hot or too cold, just as the alien visitors adapt readily to conditions on Earth.

George Adamski was able to secure fine photos of alien spacecraft because his contacts notified him in advance when they would be flying overhead.

If the contactees are somewhat vague about the method of propulsion of the alien spacecraft, this is presumably because the technology is beyond the comprehension of an average Earthperson. Canadian contactee Oscar Magocsi travelled in a "scout disc" which was able to draw up power from the Egyptian Pyramids, Inca citadels and similar places, and discharge it again in order to "charge up" sites such as Mount Shasta. George Van Tassel's contact, Singba – regional fleet authority for the entire forty-fifth projection – told him:

> Our propulsion is the transmutation of hard light particles into soft light particles. Let your scientists figure that one out.

JOURNEYS IN SPACE

Since contactees have been handpicked by the extraterrestrials, they are treated with some favour. One of their privileges is to be taken for a flight in the spacecraft, usually a brief tour in space. The especially lucky ones get to visit the aliens' own planet.

Conditions vary from one spacecraft to another. Attractive space hostesses serving delicious drinks are a recurring feature corresponding to our own practices on Earth. These always arrive without a demonstration of emergency procedures however, presumably because the idea of an emergency occurring on an extraterrestrial spacecraft is unthinkable. On the other hand, the craft are often thoughtfully equipped with elaborate equipment enabling the passenger to receive in-flight briefing on his destination.

Adamski had several flights, including a notable one which passed the Moon on the far side, enabling him to see its fauna and flora. This took place before our own first Moon landing: it is a pity our astronauts landed on the near side, which is so much less interesting.

Angelucci was taken to see his Luciferian friends' home planetoid, where Lyra and Orion explained that he too, during a previous existence, was one

Descriptions by contactees of the otherworldly places they visit, though they resemble the fantasies of fiction illustrators, are not confirmed by our own explorations of space.

Regrettably, contactees never carry cameras, nor are souvenir postcards available at the places they visit, so we have only their verbal descriptions to tell us how other worlds compare with the conceptions of fantasy illustrators.

of them. At that time an arrogant prince – also named Lucifer – almost totally destroyed the planet while rebelling against the "etheric hosts"; the planetoid they were now on was all that remained, while "the Luciferian hosts fell into the dream of mind-in-matter upon the dark planet of the sorrows" (i.e. Earth). Life

on the planetoid was of course exquisitely beautiful, and he was reluctant to return to Earth, though to comfort him they played the Bach-Gounod "Ave Maria" on the audio system.

Lee Crandall, on August 31, 1954, accepted the Venusians' invitation to

visit their planet. The flight was not too comfortable – he was airsick, which rather spoiled what would otherwise have been an enjoyable and memorable experience, particularly as he was the first Earthperson to set foot there. However, he was welcomed at a formal ceremony and invited to cooperate in

the Great Universal Endeavor of Understanding. After shaking hands all round, he returned to the spacecraft and left Venus after a stay of only 46 minutes. He developed a nasty nosebleed on the way back, but the Venusian cared for him and helped him to his mother's home. On a second visit, he saw "hundreds of beautiful feminine creatures, all blondes, all clothed in white trailing garments, floating in a swimming position". He spent seven hours there, sightseeing and enjoying a concert given by five gorgeously beautiful Venusian ladies, who looked around thirty-five years old.

Woodrow Derenberger was taken on several space journeys during the spring of 1966, including a journey past Saturn to his hosts' home planet, Lanulos. He was given an injection which enabled him to land without risk of contamination by or of the locals.

the White Sands Incident

By Daniel W. Fry

A TECHNICIAN TALKS WITH A SPACEMAN AND RIDES IN A FLYING SAUCER

As an engineer Daniel Fry appreciated the extraterrestrials' achievement when he was taken for a flight in a remotely-controlled "scout ship".

During his visit he went into shops, but was not allowed to take anything away with him. He saw that most people go nude in warm weather, and was persuaded to do likewise despite being "a little bit overweight". Otherwise, he found that life on Lanulos wasn't so very different from that on Earth: "One group of people that I met and talked to were working on a lawn. They were raking the lawn, straightening a paling fence and painting it, the same as we do here on earth". He met John and Carolyn Peterson, from Acapulco, Mexico, who emigrated to Lanulos forty years before; they told him how much they liked the life there. Derenberger himself was invited to move there with his family. "I do really want to go, but I know I can be of so much more use here on Earth".

Daniel Fry was taken for a quick half-hour flight from White Sands to New York and back at a speed averaging more than 12,000 kilometres per hour. During the flight, the distant A-lan gave him technical details, and explained that Fry was chosen for contact because he was

> one of those rare individuals whose brain receives well ... We have carefully examined the minds of many of your top scientists. In every case we found that their minds had hardened into a mould based on their present conceptions

George King's space experiences were among the most dramatic of all, for in 1956 he travelled in a material space ship while participating in a cosmic battle against a hostile planetoid whose robot inhabitants, programmed by evil forces, were scheming to wreak appalling destruction in the solar system. He was thus privileged to witness the saving of Earth from would-be destroyers.

Howard Menger was taken to the Moon, where his hosts maintained a base. This was tastefully decorated with potted plants; refreshments were served by "attractive ladies in flowing pastel gowns". A few weeks later, he flew over Venus, which was fantastically beautiful. "I did not get the impression of cities; instead, I was reminded of beautiful suburban areas I have seen on our own planet, though, of course,

wondrously [sic] different ... Vehicles moved on the surface, apparently without wheels, for they seemed to float slightly above the ground."

Could the Venusians have invented the hovercraft before us?

Hillbilly farmer Buck Nelson's extraterrestrial voyages were notable in that he was permitted to take his dog Teddy with him to Mars, the Moon, and Venus. Teddy can therefore claim to be the first earthdog in space, predating Laika, the Russian canine cosmonaut, by three years.

Reinhold Schmidt, in February and April 1958, had some interesting terrestrial trips. On one of them, he visited the Great Pyramid, entering it by a secret way. This led to a hidden room housing a 20 metre circular spacecraft, containing the cross of Jesus, the gifts of the Magi, and a crown of thorns. He learnt that this was the spaceship in which Jesus left Earth.

Claude Vorilhon, in 1975 – two years after his first encounter – was taken to visit the aliens' planet, "relatively close to Earth". It was a beautiful, paradise-like place, where the shell-like houses blended harmoniously with the natural surroundings. He attended a party, where the guests were waited on by robot servants and entertained by naked female robot dancers. The food, unusually, was not vegetarian. His host, Iahve, President of the Council of the Eternals, told him there were 8400 Earthpeople on their planet, who during their earthly lives reached a sufficiently high level of development: Iahve then pointed out Moses, Jesus and other celebrities among the guests present for the occasion.

AFTERMATH

Subsequent to their experiences, the careers of the contactees diverge considerably. Some return to their previous obscurity, while others follow up on their contact adventure in various ways.

Adamski published his account of his contact in 1953. It aroused world-wide interest, bringing fame – though probably only a modest revenue – to its author. It led to lecture tours round the globe. In Switzerland he was harassed by disbelievers, but most audiences were fascinated by his story.

Angelucci felt himself a "dweller in two worlds", and decided to devote his life to his mission, against his wife's urgings: "I'm sorry, Mae. Believe me, there is no other way out for me. I've got to live with myself". He gave Sunday afternoon talks in a California hotel, and published his story. He and his children were mocked as a result, but he didn't care because he had not failed his space visitors.

Though Bethurum had eleven meetings with lovely spacewoman Aura Rhanes, his workmates were skeptical, and his wife even more so. His daughters did back him up, however. With Adamski's support, he became a star of the contactee lecture circuit and appeared frequently on the radio. Mrs Bethurum, her doubts somewhat assuaged by his celebrity, allowed herself to be photographed smiling alongside him.

Denaerde's publisher refused to issue his account except as science fiction, and as such it was presented to the Dutch public in 1969 (where it ran through eleven editions) and later as a paperback in the United States. The editor's introduction to the Dutch edition opened with the words "Dit is geen science-fiction. Het is een utopisch boek" – literally, "This is not science fiction. It is a utopian book": but for American readers the word "exactly" is added before "science". In 1982, the story was republished in the USA as fact, though the author in his foreword remained oddly evasive:

> Though I shall continue to avoid giving a direct answer to the question of the veracity of this story, the immensity of Earth-alien knowledge contained in this book will serve to prove beyond a doubt that the planet Iarga is not fiction, but fact.

The new edition contained additional material, more than twice the bulk of the original text. Most of this was religious philosophy –lucid, explicit and ingenious – received in the form of telepathic communications every afternoon when the author got home

Desmond Leslie's 1953 book, arguing that flying saucers have existed throughout history, concluded with Adamski's account of his encounter, destined to provide a model for all subsequent contact stories.

from the office. Curiously, during this period, NATO employees in Den Haag reported being bothered by an untraceable incoming radio-frequency electronic signal, which was at its strongest in the near vicinity of Denaerde's home, and which began about 4 p.m. and continued for an hour or more several days each week – precisely when Denaerde received his messages …

When Woodrow Derenberger's story became known, he was considerably harassed by an inquisitive public, and his children were tormented at school. In August 1967 two men, dressed entirely in black, visited his store and warned him to stop talking so much about flying saucers.

> They would not identify themselves, but just said they had authority to stop me.

Aura Rhanes, captain of the alien "scow" which Truman Bethurum encountered in the Nevada desert, resembled an Earthwoman in appearance.

Woodrow Derenberger was told by two "Men in Black" to keep his experiences secret, but when he published his story he suffered no consequences.

My personal opinion is that these, and all the "men in black", are from the Mafia".

Eventually Derenberger moved to another town, but he published his story

and gave lectures about his experience. While he was participating in a "phone-in" radio program in Washington, a young man named Ed Bailey called the studio to say he too had been to Lanulos. Later the two met, in the presence of author John Keel and journalist Harold Salkin. Bailey's account confirmed Derenberger's, even including certain details which Derenberger had never publicly revealed.

Aladino Felix appeared on Brazilian TV in August 1968, and stated publicly that his book, which had been enormously successful, was outright invention. At the end of the month he was arrested for terrorist activities. He threatened the authorities that his friends on Venus would liberate him and his comrades. Undeterred, they sentenced him to 5 years imprisonment, but with the recommendation that he be transferred to an institution for mental treatment. Gordon Creighton, subsequently editor of *Flying Saucer Review*, suggested that Felix was being used as a tool by unnamed evil forces.

George King's life was changed by his encounter only in that it provided him with a specific direction for his existing interests. He gave his first public meeting in January 1955, at Caxton Hall, London. He was kept busy by his duties as representative on Earth of the Interplanetary Parliament, which was far from being a sinecure – thus in 1963, he was involved in Operation Bluewater which saved – for the time being at least – the western seaboard of the United States from imminent catastrophe. Since that was where he made his home, it must have been comforting to know his property was under extraterrestrial protection.

Menger's knowledge that he himself was a Saturnian gave him a purpose in life – "to complete a mission which had been outlined from my day of birth". In 1956, he met Marla, the sister of his childhood contact, whom he had met previously when he – then a Saturnian – had stopped over on Venus. She too was on a mission to Earth, and was conveniently now living in the next state. They resumed their interrupted love affair, marrying in 1958. He was a regular guest on radio shows, notably that of Long John Nebel, on which he made a remarkable final appearance.

Howard said nothing, and un-said most of what he had originally claimed. Where he had once sworn that he had seen flying saucers, he now felt that he had some vague impression that he might have on some half-remembered occasion possibly viewed some airborne object – maybe. Where he had once insisted that he had teleported himself, he now speculated that strange things did happen to people and if it hadn't actually occurred to him, well, that's the way the story crumbles. Where he had formerly stated that he had been to the moon, he now suggested that this had most likely been a mental impression of the other side of his consciousness. In other words, Howard Menger backed up and backed up until he fell into a pit of utter confusion and finally sank forever into the waters of obscurity.

But Nebel was mistaken. In 1991, Howard and Connie Menger re-emerged, republished their account with additions, and reaffirmed their original claims to have participated in contact with the aliens. But Menger changed his story in one respect:

Years ago, on a TV program, when I first voiced my opinion that the people I met and talked with from the craft might not be extraterrestrial, it was thought that I had recanted. However, they (the aliens) said they had just come from the planet we call Venus (or Mars). It is my opinion that these space travelers may have by-passed or visited other planets, but were not native to those planets any more than our astronauts are native to the Moon.

Several contactees formed groups or cults. Former truck-driver Kelvin Rowe published an account of his encounter in 1958. He urged a spiritual awakening of Earthfolk, which he suggested could best be accomplished via The Brotherhood of the White Temple. In addition to regular lectures and classes at its headquarters high in the Rocky Mountains, this organization "teaches by correspondence all the Secret Wisdom of the Ancients" and "gives the Degree of Doctor of Metaphysics on completion of the course".

Another contactee who became a successful cult leader was Claude

Vorilhon, who changed his name to "Raël". Following the publication of his first book in 1974, thousands attended his conferences, leading to the foundation of the Raëlian movement. has enjoyed considerable international success, largely because of its popular summer gatherings where the master's easy-going philosophy is put into uninhibited practice.

THE MESSAGES

Almost without exception, contactees believe they were chosen for their individual qualities – they are in one way or another "special". In return, they believe they have been entrusted with a mission to help Earth and its inhabitants to avoid some great disaster, or even distruction. The message given by the Great Master whom Adamski met on his February 1953 trip stands as the archetype for subsequent messages given to other contactees:

> My son, our main purpose in coming to you at this time is to warn you of the grave danger which threatens men of Earth today. Knowing more than any amongst you can yet realize, we feel it our duty to enlighten you if we can. Your people may accept the knowledge we hope to give them through you and through others, or they can turn deaf ears and destroy themselves. The choice is with the Earth's inhabitants. We cannot dictate …

Crandall's Venusians were working for peace, and with that in mind they not only asked him to transmit their warnings to mankind, but had plans to send 1000 Venusian men to land in the California desert some time in 1954, as peaceful and friendly neighbours. Venusian women lived separately from the men, there was no marriage and, seemingly, no children. "I queried if any of these women would ever come down to visit earth. I got a negative answer."

Denaerde learned that Jesus was the first of 144,000 "chosen ones" who, by the purity of their lives, would combat the evil egoism of Satan. Intelligent races on other worlds had their equivalent to our deity, but what distinguished Earthfolk was that ours

was an "own boss" culture, as opposed to the collective-mind culture of the Iargans and others.

On July 27, 1958 at Holdston Down in Devon, George King, who was heading the Aetherius Society, met the Master Jesus – who was in fact a Venusian – who gave him "the twelve blessings" which Aetherians regard as "the Bible for the Aquarian Age". Most of the doctrines were dictated by Saint Goo-Ling, a Member of the Great White Brotherhood still living on Earth. The Aetherius Society flourished to become one of the most successful of all extraterrestrial cults, with headquarters in California and branches throughout the world.

French contactee Jean Miguères was told:

> People of Earth, we have no intention of invading your world: if we wanted to, we could have done it ages ago … Our intentions are entirely peaceful; our only aim is to help you – and we warn you that you will soon need that help, for we foresee the necessity of a massive and peaceful intervention on your earth in 1996, that is, unless your stupidity doesn't make it necessary for us to step in earlier than that... You, Earthpeople, are on the point of making great discoveries, and our "Supreme Computer" warns that, thanks to them, you run the risk of destroying the entire Solar System before destroying yourself. This we cannot permit, on behalf of your galactic brothers …

Buck Nelson's Venusian visitors warned him that

> the next war, if fought, will be on American soil. America will be destroyed, then civilization all over the world will be destroyed. We have stood by and seen other planets, one other, destroy itself [sic]. Is this world next? We wonder, and watch and wait.

Siragusa learned that each of us visits Earth for seven lifetimes. He himself had formerly lived on Atlantis as Barath, a scholar; in ancient Egypt as Hermes Trismegistus; in biblical Palestine as John the Evangelist; in Renaissance Italy as Giordano Bruno; in Europe during the Enlightenment as Cagliostro; and in twentieth-century Russia as Rasputin. It was his duty to

pass this heritage of wisdom, combined with on-going teachings, to mankind. He duly formed a Study Centre of Cosmic Brotherhood, which would eventually be housed in a college on the slopes of Mount Etna – where he had his first contact. In 1978 he claimed 50,000 affiliated members, but his success was somewhat marred by scandal – mainly linked to his over-friendly relationships with young female disciples.

The public warmed to the contactees, most of whom seem to have been amiable, likeable people of disarming sincerity. They were popular on radio and TV chat shows, and were star speakers at conferences. One such regular conference was staged by George Van Tassel – himself a contactee – at Giant Rock, California. In its heyday, it attracted more than 10,000 visitors to the dramatic desert location. Did those who attended these legendary events believe what they heard? On the whole, it seems likely. A homely honesty

Buck Nelson learnt from his Venusian hosts that another war would mean the destruction of America and the end of civilization on Earth.

comes through the foreword which Fanny Lowery wrote in December 1956, for her friend Buck Nelson's account of his trip to Mars, the Moon and Venus:

> Ancient and modern history, as well as the Bible, record the visits of Space People to our planet. But now folks, the most wonderful thing is that one of our own neighbors, Buck Nelson, has actually made a trip to other planets and will now tell you about it.

Author John Keel, not easily fooled, concluded his foreword to Woodrow Derenberger's book by asking:

> Are all of these people insane? I have talked to contactee claimants who are doctors, lawyers, newspapermen, police officers and pilots. Woody has a lot of company: sane, reputable people. Perhaps we are the ones who are insane for ignoring them for so long. Strange, unbelievable things are now happening to people all over the world.

Stranger things still were to happen.

FROM CONTACT TO ABDUCTION

During the 1960s, there was a dramatic change in the nature of contact between Us and Them, between humans and extraterrestrials. From being *voluntary*, the encounters switched to being *involuntary*. The Contactees had been treated as honoured guests, invited on board the visiting space-ships, and given nice things to eat and drink. The Abductees were given no choice. They were beamed aboard spacecraft and forced to participate in medical procedures, with no word of explanation, no friendly welcome, no in-flight refreshment, and no thanks afterwards. The Contactees felt privileged: the Abductees felt used.

The contrast is in some respects so marked that those who accept abduction claims at face value – and they number a great many highly educated and intelligent people – are at pains to set them totally apart from the contact cases we have been considering so far.

A human is abducted by spaceship. Extraterrestrials become more obtrusive, taking humans from Earth for their own experimental purposes and foregoing their previous courteous behaviour.

However, the difference is by no means as clear-cut as this contrast suggests. The line of distinction between contact and abduction is a blurred one. There are many features common to both kinds of experience, which encourage us to see them as variations on one basic theme. Both involve, in the great majority of cases, solitary individuals. Both occur during the night more often than the day. Both tend to take place in isolated locations, at times when corroborative evidence would in any case be hard to find. Both happen more frequently to Americans than to anyone else, more to

North Americans than to Latin Americans, and more to Caucasians than to others. Finally, both categories rest entirely on witness testimony, unsupported by any convincing evidence.

Significantly, though, the role of the UFO itself is very different. In the contactees' stories, it figures largely in the experience. The contactee is taken on board, often treated to a conducted tour of the spacecraft, even making a journey in space. With the abductees, on the other hand, the UFO's relevance is minimal. The majority of abductees never see the spacecraft from the outside. Even the way they enter it is blurred and ambiguous. Most of them see no more of the interior than the "room" where they are examined.

The contactees prepared the way for the abductees, by attracting the world's attention to the possibility of extraterrestrial visitation. Even if they did not achieve widespread credibility, they won widespread publicity. Consequently, when the more credible abductees appeared, the public was half-way prepared to give them a serious hearing. Many wanted to believe the contactees, but found their claims too hard to swallow. When the abductees started to make their less-bizarre claims, the public turned to them in relief as being less unbelievable.

In one other respect, abduction cases do seem to be objectively different from contact cases – they seem simpler. The abduction of Betty and Barney Hill, for instance, was to all intents and purposes a one-night stand, over and done with in a few hours. This is a far cry from the complex and long-drawn-out affair of, say, Elizabeth Klarer's contact experience. On the other hand, abduction cases possess a complexity of their own, derived from the response of the individual involved. Abductees often claim a previous history of otherworldly interaction. The experience seems to affect them at a deeper level than that of contactees. To read an account by an abductee is very different from reading the old contactee books: they are more thoughtful; the experience is more profound. Does this just represent a change in the cultural climate, or is there really an essential difference between the two kinds of experience?

Abductions have split the UFO community as no other events have done. For a great many thoughtful and dedicated persons, they represent the positive event which will carry humanity from one era of history – the era when we seemed alone in the cosmos – to another era, when our destiny will merge with that of otherworldly civilizations. For psychologist Leo Sprinkle, they are part of a learning process involving the human race; for information scientist Jacques Vallee, they are part of the master-plan of a cosmic control system.

If this is true, the most important thing that has ever happened to the human race is happening right now. Why aren't governments, authorities – our leaders – taking any notice? Furthermore, why do others in the UFO community – no less thoughtful and dedicated than the believers – reject the abduction phenomenon as a collective delusion?

The fact is that though the abductees often impress listeners with their sincerity and their thoughtful response, the stories they tell are bizarre, contradictory, inconsistent and fly in the face of common sense. Moreover, though circumstantial and detailed, they are no more than personal statements – they offer no objective, material evidence, and no convincing independent confirmation.

1951: THE SALZBURG ABDUCTION

As if to emphasize the blurred distinction between contact and abduction, the event with the best claim for the status of being the first true abduction case is tantalizingly vague. In December 1957, a Canadian local newspaper, the *Prince George Citizen*, reported a story told personally to the editor by an unnamed man who in 1951 had been working for the US occupation army in Salzburg, Austria. About 11 p.m. on May 15, he was walking home from duty when he was accosted by a figure in the darkness. The figure pointed a device at him which paralysed him, then strapped some kind of "plate" on his chest. The entity pulled him, almost as if floating, to a nearby field, where a round object about 50 metres in diameter was standing:

> My thought was that a spy had captured me for some reason ... I was plenty scared.

They floated up to the top of the object, and entered through a hole. The soldier found himself in a kind of room. He was released from his paralysis, and sank to the floor:

> There was a sort of shaking sensation, and

A model alien with cylindrical head, large fly-like eliptical eyes, a small slit for a mouth and two holes for the nose. Many abductees have described their alien kidnappers as having such features.

If Earthpeople sought to colonize Mars, we would have to construct suitable habitats for ourselves;
but aliens visiting our planets seem to experience no trouble adapting to Earth conditions.

I knew the door to the room had been shut. The next sensation I had was of riding up into the air. I had never flown before in my life ... I was so scared, but I figured I was dreaming.

Suddenly, they were – unaccountably – in sunlight, and the soldier could at last see his kidnapper. The alien's head was cylindrical, with large round eyes more like a fly's than human, two holes instead of a nose, and a very small slit for a mouth. Otherwise, the being was more or less human in appearance, though somewhat shorter than the average.

The spacecraft seemed to be constructed of a translucent glass-like material. It carried them silently close to the Moon, and the soldier could see Earth far away. They then approached another planet with red fields, blue rivers, roads and bridges. They landed in a field full of other saucers like their own. The entity left him alone in the vessel and went into another ship:

I got to thinking I must be on Mars. I remembered what I had learnt in school about it being red with canals, and it seemed to me that this must be Mars, although I wasn't 100 percent sure ...

The entity then returned, and they took off again. The witness was returned to Earth, where the entity pulled him out the same way as he was pulled in, left him seemingly paralysed, and flew off. Throughout, there was no communication or contact between them. The witness ran home:

My wife was still up, and she saw me all excited. She asked me what happened and I told her, "Nothing, I'm just sick". I couldn't tell her about the experience because she would have thought I was completely crazy.

By the clock, he saw that the journey had lasted about an hour.

He explained to the editor that he was telling the story because he had a heart condition and didn't expect to live much longer, and felt people should know what was going on.

Those people are much ahead of us ... this creature treated me only as an animal.

Unsatisfactory though it is in almost every respect, the Salzburg case is of interest because it predates any other abduction story. The account of being floated through the air occurs again in later reports, but for earlier instances we would have to turn to fairytales. Similarly, the immobilizing device resembles that used in a famous case near Valensole, France, in 1965 when a farmer reported being immobilized by aliens. This, however, took place eight years after the Salzburg incident was published.

Where the aliens come from, and how they travel to Earth, is hard to determine: here, the abductors of
Barney and Betty Hill show them a "star map" depicting their journey.

1961:
BARNEY AND BETTY HILL

The case which for many years set the pattern for abductions was that of Barney and Betty Hill, which presented virtually every feature – and raised virtually every question – of the entire abduction phenomenon.

In 1961, Barney and Betty Hill were living in Portsmouth, New Hampshire. Barney, a thirty-nine-year old man, worked as a Post Office sorter, a job rather below his intellectual capacity. He was also an active campaigner for civil rights. His wife Betty, forty-one, was a child welfare worker. Both had been married previously; they were popular and had many friends. Their inter-racial marriage, though sometimes inconvenient, was happy and caused them no obvious tension.

On the night of September 19, 1961, the couple were returning home after a short spur-of-the-moment vacation in Canada, driving through the night because their funds were running low. They stopped for a snack at a roadside restaurant, leaving a little after 10 p.m. What happened then is recounted in a letter Betty wrote six days later to Donald Keyhoe – a prominent UFO investigator whose book *The Flying Saucer Conspiracy* she found in a local library:

> My husband and I have become immensely interested in this topic, as we recently had quite a frightening experience, which does seem to differ from others of which we are aware. About midnight on September 20th we were driving in a National Forest area in the White Mountains. This is a desolate, uninhabited area. We noticed a bright object in the sky which seemed to be moving rapidly. We stopped our car and got out to observe it more closely with our binoculars. Suddenly it reversed its flight path and appeared to be flying in a very erratic pattern. We continued driving. As it approached our car, we stopped again. As it hovered in the air in front of us, it appeared to be pancake in shape, ringed with windows in the front through

which we could see bright blue-white lights. My husband was standing in the road, watching closely. He saw wings on each side and red lights on the wing tips.

> As it glided closer he was able to see inside this object, but not too closely. He did see several figures scurrying about as though they were making some hurried type of preparation. One figure was observing us from the windows. At this point my husband became shocked and got back in the car in a hysterical condition, laughing and repeating that they were going to capture us. As we started to move, we heard several buzzing or beeping sounds which seemed to be striking the trunk of our car.

At that stage, there was no more to the case than a fairly dramatic UFO sighting – alarming enough to the witnesses, but nothing more. Then, for five successive nights, starting on September 30, Betty experienced disturbing dreams in which their sighting, instead of ending when they got back into the car, continued with a series of dramatic events. In Betty's dream, the Hills unaccountably found themselves on a different road from the one on which they had been travelling. They came across a group of figures standing in the middle of the road. Barney slowed down and the motor died. The figures surrounded the car, opened the car doors, took Barney and Betty by the arms and led them along a path through the woods to where a spaceship was parked. They were taken inside and led to separate rooms, where they were stripped and subjected to what seemed to be a medical examination. The entities were not unfriendly, and the experience was not especially unpleasant. The leader apologized to Betty for frightening her. She was then reunited with Barney, and they were led back through the woods to their car. Betty by now was talking with the leader, saying she was happy to meet him and begging him to return.

On October 21, Walter Webb – an investigator for NICAP, Keyhoe's UFO organization – visited the Hills and heard about the sighting, though not the dreams. He reported:

> It is the opinion of this investigator, after questioning these people for over six hours and studying their reactions and

The abduction of Betty and Barney Hill took place after they had stopped to observe a low-flying UFO.

personalities during that time, that they were telling the truth, and the incident occurred exactly as reported except for some minor uncertainties.

Significantly, he added:

> Mr Hill believes he saw something he doesn't want to remember. He claimed he was not close enough to see any facial characteristics on the figures [the ones seen in the UFO, not those encountered in the dreams], although at another time he referred to one of them grinning … It is my view that the observer's blackout is not of any great significance. I think the whole experience was so improbable and fantastic to witness – along with the very real fear of being captured added to imagined fears – that his mind finally refused to believe what his eyes were perceiving and a mental block resulted.

On November 25, during the course of a second meeting with NICAP investigators, a curious anomaly emerged. Barney reported:

They [the investigators] were mentally reconstructing the trip. One of them said, "What took you so long to get home? You went this distance and it took you these hours: where were you?" I thought I was really going to crack up … I realized for the first time that at the rate of speed I always travel, we should have arrived home at least two hours earlier than we did.

Accounts of the event often give the impression that the Hills noted their "missing time" as soon as they got home. This was not the case. Another feature which has often been misinterpreted in the interest of heightened drama is the allegation that they "unaccountably" turned onto a side road – the implication being that the aliens somehow brainwashed them into leaving the highway onto a totally wrong road. But the map shows that Route 175 – the one they took – runs almost parallel to Route 3, the one they wanted. Travelling at night, it would be easy to take the other road which, as it happens, was a perfectly reasonable alternative.

Such details as these – unimportant in themselves – warn us that a mythmaking process may be at work.

During February 1962 and the following months, the Hills made a series of "pilgrimages" to the scene of their experience. Then on March 12, on NICAP's suggestion, Betty inquired about the possibility of using hypnosis to help clarify what happened to them:

The moment they suggested hypnosis, I thought of my dreams, and this was the first time I began to wonder if they were more than just dreams. I thought, if I have hypnosis, I'll know one way or the other, because I thought, well, maybe my dreams are something that really happened.

A doctor listened sympathetically, but discouraged them from doing anything at the time. During the summer of 1962, Barney developed physical and psychological symptoms that forced him to seek medical help. As his condition deteriorated, they decide to try hypnosis after all, and were recommended to approach Dr Benjamin Simon, an experienced and open-minded practitioner. On January 4, 1964, seven months of hypnosis sessions commenced. It is important to realize that the purpose of the hypnosis was to see what relevance the alleged UFO sighting might have had to Barney's health, physical and mental. Moreover, the sessions were carried out entirely at the Hills' own instigation, at what must have been very considerable expense for a couple in their modest circumstances. Their motivation was evidently strong.

Each was hypnotized separately, with the other out of the room. Neither heard the recordings of either his or her own session or the other's, until the whole series of sessions was completed.

The record revealed that each, independently, had told a story which matched Betty's troubling dreams in

Dr Simon emphasized that the events "'recalled" under hypnosis by Betty and Barney Hill were only the truth as they felt and understood it, not necessarily objective truth.

detail, except that each described the events as seen from his or her own viewpoint. It was not surprising that many jumped to the obvious conclusion – that the Hills had undergone an experience so alarming that they couldn't face it. Instead, observers reasoned, they had repressed the memory of it, and it then emerged subconsciously in Betty's dreams and Barney's psychogenic troubles. The hypnosis had brought the repressed memories to light.

Attractive as this scenario is, it is invalidated by the fact that apparent memories which emerge during hypnosis cannot be taken at face value. Dr Simon himself pointed out:

> The charisma of hypnosis has tended to foster the belief that hypnosis is the magical and royal road to *truth*. In one sense this is so, but it must be understood that hypnosis is a pathway to the truth as it is felt and understood by the patient … this may or may not be consonant with the ultimate nonpersonal truth.

It is often assumed that Barney's sickness was due to anxiety caused by their experience. Apart from the fact that at that point the experience was thought to be only a UFO sighting – dramatic enough, no doubt, but less dramatic by a long way than the abduction encounter of which they were at that stage unaware – Barney was ill before the incident. What happened in 1962 was not that he developed an ulcer, but that the ulcer from which he was already suffering grew worse. The UFO experience could more plausibly have been a consequence of his state than the cause of it.

Betty, too, may have been preconditioned. Her sister Janet and many other members of the family had experienced UFO sightings. Moreover, she had a history of psychic experiences in her family, including poltergeist phenomena and precognitive *dreams*.

Perhaps the most serious question, though, is that raised by the similarity of the hypnotically revealed story to the dream-story. As we all know, dreams rarely present a literal playback of real-life events. When such events occur, they are generally re-worked, distorted, and combined with other kinds of material.

The fact that the Hills' hypnosis-recall exactly matched Betty's dream-story suggests that what they recalled under hypnosis was not the event itself, but the dreams.

So how did Barney's hypnosis-story come to match Betty's? Because he was recalling the dreams she had narrated to him, not his own personal experiences. Dr Simon himself, though he was discreet enough to never commit himself to a specific assessment, evidently favoured some such version as this:

> I was ultimately left with the conclusion that the most tenable explanation was that the series of dreams experienced by Mrs Hill, as the aftermath of some type of experience with an Unidentified Flying Object or some similar phenomenon, assumed the quality of a fantasized experience.

The Hill case is important not only in its own right, but because it served as the yardstick by which other abduction experiences would be judged. In particular, the idea of recall under hypnosis – previously regarded with some hesitation as a tool which occasionally produced useful therapeutic results – became the treatment of choice for abduction witnesses. Not until the 1990s would the shortcomings and dangers of reliance on hypnosis be recognized, and even then not by all.

1967: BETTY ANDREASSON

If abduction stories are an accurate narration of what actually took place, then what Betty Andreasson experienced on January 25, 1967 was bizarre indeed.

That evening, Betty was with her seven children and her parents at their family home in South Ashburnham, Massachusetts. Her husband had been in hospital for more than a month, as the result of a car accident.

Around 6.30 p.m. the house lights flickered and went out. Soon after, a pulsating pink light appeared outside the kitchen window. Her father went to investigate, and saw strange creatures he likened to "Hallowe'en freaks". Betty sent all her family into the living room, while she remained in the kitchen. She was thus the only one to see four creatures enter the house, passing through the closed kitchen door; they moved "in a jerky motion, leaving a vapory image behind".

Unfortunately, how much of the experience Betty was able to remember consciously is not clear from the accounts we have. Clearly though, she remembered enough to believe she had experienced an encounter with UFO occupants, because in 1974 she responded to an invitation from the *National Enquirer* for UFO stories. The fact that she was a reader of this particular paper – known more for its enthusiasm than for an unshakeable

Betty Andreasson believed she was entertaining angels when extraterrestrials appeared to her having passed through a solid door.

attachment to literal truth – is in itself an indication of possible preconditioning. However, the *Enquirer* was not interested in her story.

Betty later contacted UFO organizations and, after some delay, her case was passed to veteran investigator Raymond Fowler. It was decided that hypnosis was needed to release Betty's hidden memories. She agreed, and under hypnosis was able to tell a richer and more dramatic story.

It started with an odd but revealing assumption. Because she was a devout Christian, Betty jumped to the conclusion that because her visitors were able to pass through a solid door, they must have been angels. They didn't look like traditional angels though, any more than they looked like people, having huge pear-shaped heads, Mongoloid faces, slanting eyes and three-fingered hands.

However, she was reassured by their air of friendliness, and was no longer frightened. The lights came back on. Recalling the Biblical phrase about "entertaining angels", she asked with characteristic American hospitality if they were hungry, and when they nodded, she started to prepare food for them. But there was evidently some misunderstanding, for they rejected what she offered.

Everyone else, apart from Betty, had been put into a state of suspended animation, though nine-year old Becky was momentarily revived, to reassure Betty that the others were alright.

A typical incident during an abduction – the aliens insert an implant in the victim's nose.

Under hypnosis, Becky was able to recall seeing her mother speaking with the visitors. When Betty questioned her visitors, a bizarre but revealing conversation followed.

Betty asked "What are you doing here?" and their leader, who told her he was named Quazgaa, replied

> "We have come to help.
> Will you help us?"
> "How can I help?" asked Betty.
> "Would you follow us?"
> "Are you of God? You keep saying you have come to help the world. Why?"
> "Because the world is trying to destroy itself."
> "How can I help the world?"

The visitors repeatedly answered "Would you follow us?" to her questions, until eventually she agreed to go with them.

The visitors floated her out through the door to where their spacecraft was parked outside. As they looked at it, the bottom became transparent. Inside the spacecraft, she was given a complex and painful medical examination. This involved removing a small buckshot-like object from her nose and inserting probes through her navel. Some of the things they did to her indicated concern for her comfort, but the overall experience was distinctly unpleasant.

After the examination, Betty was taken to "a higher place" with tunnels and huge rooms, where she had what seemed to be some kind of mystical experience. She was then returned home.

This bald summary gives no more than a sampling of Betty's story, which – with its complexities and sequels – fills five volumes of meticulous narration and analysis by Fowler. There is, for instance, the ever-present religious aspect. Betty herself was a strong fundamentalist Christian, and spent much time reading the Bible. The phrase "Follow me" certainly sounds like an echo of Jesus gathering his disciples. Fowler, who himself converted to Christianity in 1952, asked the hypnotized Betty:

> "Have they anything to do with what we call the second coming of Christ?"
> "They definitely do."

> "When is this going to occur?"
> "It is not for them to tell you."
> "Do they know?"
> "They know the Master is getting ready, and very close."

Hypnosis also revealed a considerable history of previous events, going back to when, at the age of seven, Betty seems to have had her first contact. She suffered a "sting", which may have been the implanting of some monitoring device between her eyes – perhaps the one which was removed during her 1967 experience. She also heard a voice telling her "they have been watching me, and, ah, I'm coming along fine", and that they would be back in five years' time.

Indeed she had another encounter – aged twelve– with a being who emerged, like the White Rabbit, from a hole in the ground while she was out in the woods. It resembled her 1967 visitors. Again she heard voices discussing her, and one said "She's got another year".

A year later they were back, and this time they took her somewhere (later we learn it was the same "higher place" that she was taken to in 1967) and gave her a medical examination. Further contacts were reported at age eighteen and age twenty-four, seeming to confirm Fowler's suggestion that "a race or races of aliens have a long-term interest in certain members of our species, for some unknown purpose". There was a clear inference that they selected Betty Aho (as she then was) as a child, and monitored her throughout her life, checking up on her at intervals, notably at puberty and shortly after the birth of her first child.

The sexual connotations of the case, too, are inescapable. Much of the imagery of her abduction is susceptible to a sexual interpretation. The probing of her navel was read by psychoanalyst Ernest Taves as a "displacement" for the vagina, and there was much more beside. Taves rightly pointed out that a satisfactory investigation would have elicited much more about the sexual and religious aspects of Betty's personality and situation. At the same time, we can understand that whereas a psychoanalyst such as Taves might feel it essential to explore such avenues, a hard-headed UFO investigator like

Fowler might feel diffident about treading on such delicate ground. Similarly, Fowler, himself a believing Christian, might not have been inclined to question the religious aspects.

Taves posed the question:

Which is the simpler, more reasonable, more rational explanation of this exotic adventure: (1) Betty was taken aboard an extragalactic spacecraft by aliens who have been visiting Earth since the beginning of time but haven't been able to effect meaningful communication with man. (2) Betty recalled, or relived, in hypnosis, a dream or fantasy (or a number of them) that had meaning and utility in terms of her life history and her emotional needs?

For Taves, sitting at home reviewing Fowler's book, the answer was self-evident. For Fowler, who lived through the sessions which led to the writing of the books and who in the course of his investigation came to realize that he was himself an abductee, it was the opposite conclusion which imposes itself. "The witnesses believed it happened. And so, for that matter, do I".

1973:
CHARLES HICKSON AND CALVIN PARKER

Charles Hickson (aged forty-two) and Calvin Parker (nineteen) were fishing on a riverbank at Pascagoula, Mississippi, on October 11. Around 7 p.m. (or 9 p.m. in later versions) they saw a bright object descend behind them, about 20 metres away. It resolved into a craft about 3 metres in diameter (or 7 to 10 metres in later versions) which landed. Three creatures emerged from it. They were classic alien entities – shorter than humans, pale grey colour, wrinkled skin, two-fingered hands, small ears. The eyes however – usually a

prominent feature – were almost invisible in the folds of their wrinkled skin, if indeed they possessed eyes at all.

The two men sat unable to move as the beings approached them. Hickson had the impression that Parker fainted with fright, and this was Parker's own

impression. Under subsequent hypnosis however, Parker was able to recall being carried into the ship. Hickson had a conscious memory of being seized by two of the creatures, and together they floated towards the UFO.

Hickson found himself in a fiercely

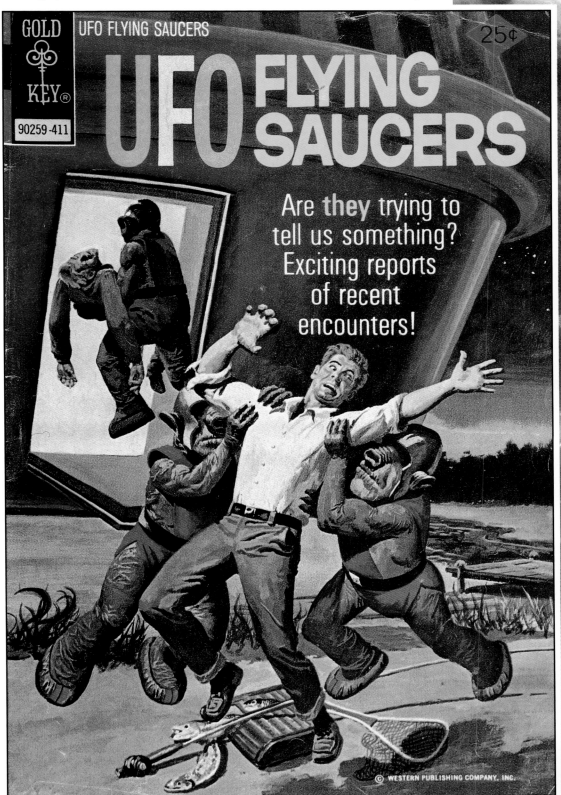

The Pascagoula incident was sufficiently dramatic to justify this illustration: the men were not politely invited, but forcibly taken on board the spacecraft.

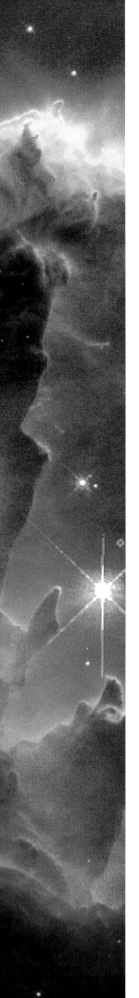

brightly-lit room. He couldn't see Parker, and assumed he had been taken elsewhere. Alone, he was given some kind of physical examination. Then the two men were floated out of the spacecraft and left on the riverbank, Parker still unconscious. The creatures floated back to their craft, which took off and disappeared, leaving an unspoken, seemingly telepathic message: "We are peaceful, we meant you no harm".

The two men went that very evening to tell their story to the local sheriff, who recorded it. They hoped to avoid publicity, but the media got to hear of it somehow, and by the next day their story had spread across the world. Their account was wildly and irresponsibly sensationalized, and when the men successfully underwent a lie detector test, there was a widespread impression not only that the event really happened as told, but that it had been scientifically validated.

Hickson reported additional contacts and psychic experiences subsequent to their experience. Subsequent investigation included hypnosis sessions which added fresh material. but also opened up new questions.

1975:
TRAVIS WALTON

On the November 5, seven men had spent the day cutting wood in the Apache-Sitgreaves National Forest, Arizona. They were preparing to go home at 6.10 p.m. when their truck rounded a bend in the forest track and they saw a glowing structured object about 30 metres ahead of them, hovering some 5 metres above the ground.

Travis Walton (aged twenty-two) shouted to the driver to stop, jumped out, hurried towards the object, and stood looking at it. It was a classic "one-shallow-bowl-inverted-on-another" UFO, seemingly some 5 metres in diameter. His companions shouted to him to be careful, and to come back. He stepped back two paces and a blue-green beam shot out from the bottom of the craft. It struck him, lifted him into the air and threw him back onto the ground.

Believing that they were all in

danger, the leader drove away rapidly with the five others. After travelling some 400 metres, they stopped. Looking back, they saw a light rise from the ground which they assumed to be the object. Somewhat ashamed of their flight, they drove back to the clearing, but there was no sign of Walton. After searching in vain, they drove to the nearest town, Heber, and informed the Sheriff.

Next they informed Walton's family. When his mother heard the news, "she did not act very surprised, she said "Well, that's the way these things happen". His sister, too, took the news surprisingly calmly.

The following morning, some fifty persons took part in a thorough but fruitless search. There were no signs of the UFO at the alleged site. Late in the afternoon, his mother said "I don't think there is any use of looking any further. He's not around here. I don't think he's on this earth". His brother Duane, in an interview, expressed no fear for Walton's well-being. because he was convinced Walton was alive and well in a flying saucer. The brothers had discussed the subject many times, and had agreed that if the opportunity presented itself, "we would immediately get as directly under the object as physically possible" in hope of being taken up. His only regret

"Well, that's the way these things happen," was Travis Walton's mother's philosophical comment when she heard that her son had been abducted by aliens.

was that it was Travis, not he, who was "having the experience of a lifetime".

Because the police had to consider the possibility of foul play, Walton's co-workers took polygraph tests which seemed to confirm that they were telling the truth. Five days after his disappearance, at around midnight, Walton called the only member of the family with a phone, his brother in law, from a payphone in a gas station in Heber. The brother in law picked up Duane and drove to Heber. There, they found Walton slumped in the phone booth, unshaven and looking thin.

Under hypnosis, Walton recalled a more-or-less stereotype abduction experience, including a physical examination in what he took to be a hospital, conducted by short pale thin aliens with oversize heads, large eyes and seamless clothing. When he resisted them, his examiners left the room. He went wandering round the premises, visiting other rooms and meeting other aliens who forced him onto a table where he lost consciousness. These memories seemed to cover only a period of about an hour. When he recovered consciousness he was lying on the ground near a highway. He saw the spacecraft, in which he had presumably been for five days, flying away.

The Walton case is unique in that there were six witnesses who saw the spacecraft and the beam of light. Unless they were conspiring with him to deceive, it seems that the mysterious object – though not necessarily an alien spacecraft – and his five-day absence – though not necessarily on board the craft – are matters of fact.

Grounds for doubting the physical reality of the abduction have been demonstrated by Philip Klass, who has unearthed a mass of circumstantial detail which other investigators had either failed to find or chosen to disregard. Klass established that not only Walton but all his family were obsessed with the idea of going aboard a UFO. He also pointed to countless discrepancies, contradictions and outright lies in the testimony.

Yet we must set against this the fact that today, even after more than 20 years, Walton and his companions are still sticking firmly to their story. In 1996, he reissued his original account,

replying at length to Klass's criticisms. Ostensibly, Walton is as believable as his story is unbelievable.

1976: Louise Smith, Mona Stafford and Elaine Thomas

Though multiple abductions have been reported at other times, in most cases those involved are couples like the Hills, parents with children like Betty Andreasson, or two close friends like Hickson and Parker. In this case however, the abductees were three ladies, aged 44, 35 and 48 respectively. Each lived independently of the others, though they enjoyed a close friendship based on shared artistic interests.

On January 6, they were driving home after a late dinner when all three saw a strange object in the sky, seemingly a typical domed-disc UFO. This seemed to affect their control of the car. They also saw luminous phenomena which, when they got home, had affected their eyes and skin. They also noted that their journey seemed to

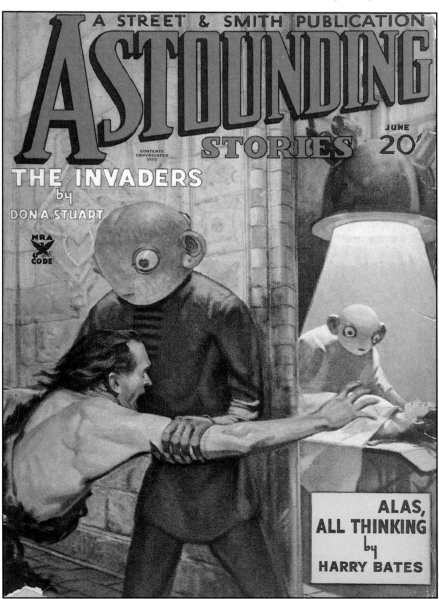

The physical examination of humans by aliens – a standard feature of abduction stories – was anticipated by the creators of science fiction such as this tale from 1935.

A portrait of an alien kidnapper with the hysterically screaming image of the abductee mirrored in his eyes.

have taken some 90 minutes longer than they would have expected.

They reported their experience to UFO investigators. Under hypnosis, each had an abduction tale to tell. The space ship took the car – with its three occupants – up into itself. The aliens separated the three, and took Stafford onto a different spaceship, which gave her the feeling of being "in a cave or volcano – underground somewhere". Both she and Smith described being subjected to a painful physical examination by grey, hooded aliens, about 1.5 metres (3 ½ ft) tall, with large eyes slanting towards the temples.

Dr Leo Sprinkle, who examined them, favoured a face-value interpretation:

> Although it is not possible to claim absolutely that a physical examination and abduction have taken place, I believe that this is the best hypothesis to explain the apparent loss-of-time experience and the apparent physical and emotional reactions.

Those who investigated the case were all impressed by the testimony, and shared Sprinkle's acceptance. However, some details do seem to warrant notice.

There were long-term personality changes in the witnesses, and mystical overtones. Both Stafford and Thomas had subsequent experiences. A few weeks before her death – which occurred shortly after the incident, though there is no reason to suppose a connection – Thomas noticed that her home was being "watched" by a UFO which sometimes slowly approached the house. Stafford found an alien in her trailer kitchen one evening who spoke to her enigmatically, then left.

Louise Thomas had purchased the car in which the three had their experience that very day. People buy cars all the time, and Americans more than most, but it is still a curious coincidence that a car which seemed to go out of control should be an unfamiliar vehicle which its new owner was driving at night for the very first time.

As chance would have it, it was Mona Stafford's birthday. Again, on average, 1 in 365 abductees is liable to have a birthday abduction; nevertheless, we must ask ourselves whether – as seemed likely in the case of contactee Eugenio Siragusa – the occasion may have had a special significance?

Both Smith and Stafford lived in trailers. Though this is more common in the United States than in Europe, it does imply a somewhat rootless personal life. Smith was a widow and Stafford a divorcee. Thomas was married.

All three were notably devout churchgoers. Though this is the rule rather than the exception in the United States, it is also a reminder that they subscribe to a belief system which may have had a part in shaping their experience.

These are trivial points, no doubt, and if the circumstances of their experience were more solidly rooted, it would seem trivial to raise them. But the fact is that their experience was far from being solidly rooted. Their stories were more like dream impressions than detailed memories. They did not seem to share the same experience, and there were subjective aspects to their stories which are hard to account for if it was an objective reality. A curious feature was noted, though without comment, by the Lorenzens in their account:

> Certain similarities were observed: a feeling of anxiety on the part of each witness regarding a specific aspect of the experience. For Ms Smith, it was the "wall" and the "gate" beyond which she was afraid to "move" psychologically; for Ms Stafford it was the "eye" which she had observed and the impression that something evil or bad would be learned if she allowed the eye to "control" her; for Ms Thomas, it was the "blackness" which seemed to be the feared condition or cause for anxiety.

Just what this means, and indeed what may have been significant about any of the various features, we can only guess. However, they add a further dimension of mystery to a very mysterious incident.

1978 AND OTHER TIMES: DEBBIE JORDAN

New York artist Budd Hopkins has been investigating abduction experiences since 1975, and the three books he has written about his work make an impressive case for the physical reality and extraterrestrial origin of these experiences. It is a case made all the stronger by the fact that Hopkins is well aware of the objections to this viewpoint, and insists that he has come to espouse it only because his first-hand work with scores of witnesses has convinced him that it is the one tenable position.

Between 1976 and 1981, when his first book *Missing Time* was published, Hopkins was:

> involved to varying degrees with the investigation of nineteen similar abduction cases involving thirty-seven people. These nineteen cases have yielded clear patterns ... it seems to me as if these quite similar abductions constitute some kind of systematic "research" program,

American artist Budd Hopkins has become the leading investigator of abduction cases and is a staunch believer in the literal truth of the accounts.

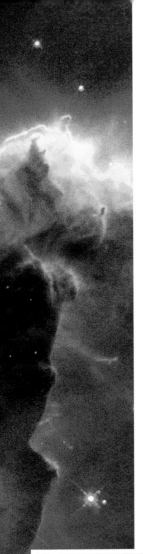

with the human species as subject. Individuals or small groups of people are involuntarily "borrowed", and most often the memory of such an encounter is effectively erased from the individual's consciousness ... What the purposes of these temporary abductions are, and what part of the experience may be purely psychic, we can only guess, but that they have a physical dimension seems to me beyond doubt ...Several abductees bear scars on their bodies from incisions made years earlier when the subjects had been children ... I have heard these witnesses, under hypnosis, describe in almost exactly the same words the equipment used to make these incisions.

From the seven cases he narrates, these similarities emerge clearly and forcefully, and it would be easy to share his conclusion that "extraterrestrials have been observing us in our innocence for many years., they are already here". This conclusion was only confirmed by the Debbie Jordan ("Kathie Davis") case, an account which he published in 1987.

The story was immensely complicated, and made more so – as he himself acknowledges – because he narrated the details in the order he learned them. What was distinctive about the Jordan case was the on-going character of the events, giving the impression that Debbie was living two lives at once – her conscious Earthly existence, and one which emerged only under hypnosis, but whose events intertwined with her consciously lived life. In the following brief summary, the bracketed events are those recalled only subsequently, under hypnosis, during Hopkins' investigation.

In 1947, Debbie's sister Kathy was born; when she was two years old, her mother had a strange dream in which she hid Kathy from two men who were in the house to take her away. Later, they surmised that this possibly concealed an abduction.

Debbie was born in 1958, and almost from birth suffered from ill-health. She was treated for high blood pressure. During childhood she suffered from hepatitis, pneumonia, hypoglycaemia, hyperadrenalism and various allergies: her appendix was removed, along with cysts on her ovaries. She had traction for two extra vertebrae which became fused. She was chronically overweight, seemingly due to hormonal imbalance.

Debbie suffered from chronic anxiety and had strange dreams. Around the age of eight, she had a dreamlike experience of visiting a strange house where a strange child plays a strange game, giving her a scar which she still possesses. At one point, he seemed to turn into a small, large-headed grey-skinned entity.

In July 1975, visiting a state park, Debbie saw strange lights and had a weird encounter with three strange men. In December, driving around the countryside with friends, they saw UFOs and stopped to look. (Years later, under hypnosis, she recalled being taken into a landed UFO and subjected to a gynaecological operation.)

Debbie was "sexually active" but, though ignorant of contraception, had been lucky enough not to become pregnant. About this time she met and fell in love with her husband-to-be. They planned to marry in mid-1978. When she found herself pregnant, they planned to marry sooner. In March Debbie was shattered – and her doctor surprised – to find she was no longer pregnant. (In subsequent hypnotic recall, she remembered being abducted and having her unborn child surgically removed.)

In April she married. That summer, living in a suburb of Indianapolis, she had an extremely vivid "dream" of seeing two strange figures in her bedroom. One was holding a small black box which he handed to her, telling her that "when the time is right you will see it again, you will remember and you'll know how to use it". Her family remember her telling them about the dream. In July her boy was born, two months prematurely, by caesarean section, because of a kidney failure.

In 1980, pregnant with her second son, Debbie received strange phone calls around the same time on Wednesday afternoons over a period of several months, until her baby was born. No words were spoken, just weird sounds. She changed her phone number to an unlisted number; a few minutes after getting the new number, the mysterious caller called on the new number, sounding angry. The mother and a friend each took one such call and confirmed this. In September her second child was born: he grew up with a speech problem, and made sounds

Many abductees speak of "missing time"; minutes – sometimes hours – that they are unable to account for.

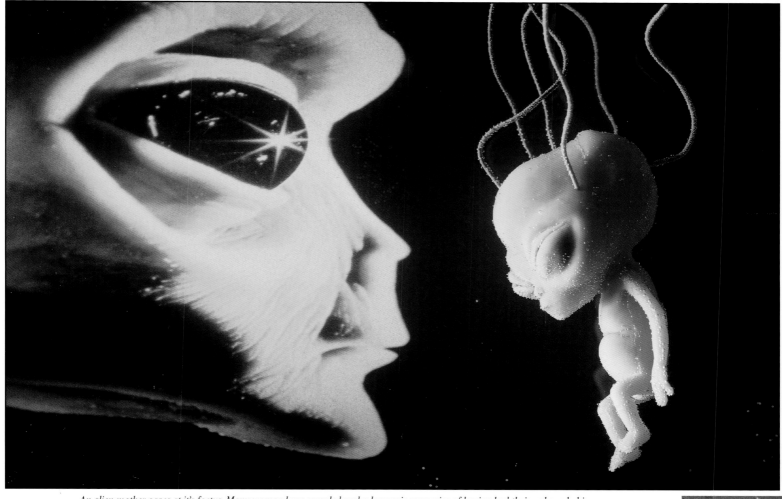

An alien mother gazes at it's foetus. Many woman have revealed under hypnosis memories of having had their unborn babies surgically removed while held prisoner by alien beings.

closely resembling the mysterious telephone caller.

In 1981 Debbie divorced and went to live with her parents. One night in 1983 her mother saw a ball of light around their property. Quite a lot of coming and going took place, but adding up all the times, it seems there was an hour unaccounted for in Debbie's time. The next morning they found mysterious traces on the lawn, which were clearly visible two years later.

Debbie read Hopkins' recently published book *Missing Time* and recognized similarities between the cases he described therein and her own experiences; so in August she wrote to him, and eventually met and was investigated by him. On October 3, as subsequently recalled under hypnosis, she encountered an alien entity while driving to the store. (Later, she was taken from her bedroom to a UFO where she was shown a small child. She recalled

that an entity visited the Jordan home, paralysed the older child and seemingly placed a nasal implant in the younger child; she herself was abducted again.)

In 1984–5, she had dreams of being pregnant. In 1986, she was wakened by her older child who has been frightened by a strange light: Debbie then saw an entity walk past her door from the younger child's room. In April she had a dream – perhaps concealing an abduction – in which she was shown a tiny baby, and told that it, and the small girl she saw 1983, are two of nine children born from ova removed from her in 1978.

Assembled in this way, the incidents in Debbie's life seem to form a consistent and plausible story in which she is used as breeding stock by visiting extraterrestrials. But if this is true, it is a story unlike that of any other abductee or contactee. There is virtually nothing to her experience except matters of

pregnancy and childbirth.

We are asked to believe, however, that – having the entire human race at their disposal – the aliens chose Debbie Jordan, with her obvious ill-health, anxieties and associated problems, to be the parent of their experimental offspring. Alternatively, if they had some special reason for using her, why didn't they give her the benefit of their scientific expertise and cure some of her ailments, as we have seen aliens do in other cases?

In 1994, Debbie Jordan and her sister Kathy Mitchell published their own account of their experiences. It continued the saga of extraordinary incidents: opening the book at random, we read that Debbie was in her current (third) husband's bathroom when the toilet paper roll suddenly unwound spontaneously, almost to the end. This is not the sort of way we would generally expect otherworldly visitors to indicate their presence.

Observers and Operators

✫

For tens of thousands of American citizens, the future is already present. The science fiction that was a dream for their grandfathers has become a real-life nightmare. The alien invaders, that writer H.G. Wells warned them about, are currently visiting Earth's air-space. Tonight and every night, they will enter victims' bedrooms, carry them up to their spacecraft on beams of light, and perform sinister surgical operations on them before returning them to their beds. Whether they know it or not, whether they like it or not, whether they believe it or not, the victims can do nothing to stop it.

David Jacobs, Associate Professor of History at Temple University, Philadelphia, takes a pessimistic, not to say alarmist, view of the proliferation of abduction claims:

> The evidence clearly indicates that the aliens are conducting a widespread, systematic program of physiological exploitation of human beings …
> Everything the aliens do is logical, rational, and goal-oriented …
> They are engaging in the systematic and clandestine physiological exploitation, and perhaps alteration, of human beings for the purposes of passing on their genetic capabilities to progeny who will integrate into the human society and, without doubt, control it.
> Their agenda is self-centred.

Not everyone takes so negative a view of alien abductions. Pessimists and optimists alike agree, however, that abductions are the indication that there is a massive, planned operation in progress, which will profoundly affect the future of the human race. This could be the most important thing to ever happen to humanity, but the authorities seem oblivious to the implications.

Something is certainly happening.

The crazed fear that afflicts the abducted as they are forced into alien surroundings and confronted with the unknown.

Twenty years ago, scarcely anyone was claiming to have made personal contact with extraterrestrials. Today, if we can believe those who have made a study of such things, abductees are numbered in tens of thousands. The leading investigator into abductions, American artist Budd Hopkins, claims to have investigated 1500 cases – and he made that claim in 1993. He is far from being the only investigator with a substantial case-file, to say nothing of the countless cases that haven't surfaced because the witnesses chose not to report them, or were not even aware that they ever took place. One of the characteristics of abductions is that often they do not come to light until long after the event, when some other circumstance reveals them by chance.

In 1992 a poll was carried out which seemed to show that millions of Americans may have been abducted by aliens from other worlds. If we can believe the findings of the Roper Poll, the probable total for the United States alone is 3.7 million. This suggests that – unless the USA is being specifically targeted – anywhere between 16 and 200 million (depending on how you interpret the figures) have been abducted world-wide. Even if we take the lowest estimate, 16 million is a lot of people. And that figure does not include the millions of 'Star People' living among us; those who maintain they originate from planets other than the Earth.

Furthermore, it is rare for an abductee to have just the one experience. Barney and Betty Hill were unusual in this respect. Most of those who Jacobs has questioned claim repeated abductions. Gloria Kane was abducted 54 times during the 8 months between July 1988 and February 1989, in November-December 1993 Kay Summers was abducted 14 times in a single month, and 38-year old Charles Petrie has consciously remembered more than 200 abductions – and counting.

Such figures should certainly justify the claims that a mighty change is taking place in humankind's interaction with the Cosmos. Yet, paradoxically, there is no convincing evidence that any of these

Though Earth scientists monitor nearby space round-the-clock, they have never detected an extraterrestrial intruder.

events are taking place at all, and there are many reasons to question whether there is any otherworldly involvement whatsoever. Each and every one of those abductions was, ostensibly, a material and therefore observable event taking place in our Earthly air-space, yet none has been reliably witnessed by passers-by, police patrols, aircraft, or whoever.

The absence of physical evidence and of confirmatory testimony is often explained away on the grounds that abductions occur on some other level of reality than the here-and-now level of what we term "reality". But as we saw earlier, the "abductions-are-real" agenda of Hopkins, Jacobs and fellow abductionists requires that there are physical explanations for such phenomena as humans passing through walls, being impregnated and so on. If abductions really happen, they happen within the same kind of reality as that in which you and I go out of our homes or become pregnant.

THE IMAGINARY ABDUCTEE EXPERIMENTS

In 1977, Professor Alvin Lawson and Dr W C McCall carried out a unique experiment in a hospital at Anaheim California. Having investigated a number of alleged abduction cases, Lawson was puzzled by various

"True" abductee Judy Kendall draws her abduction for Alvin Lawson and Dr McCall; her experience matched that of the "imaginary abductees".

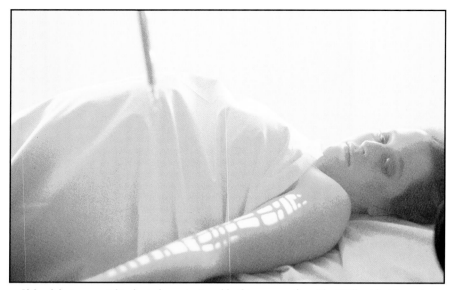

If the abductees are right, physical examinations like this – a scene from The X-Files *television series – are taking place every night in our skies.*

ambiguous indications, and suspected that some of his witnesses, though plausible and seemingly sincere, had not actually experienced the abduction they claimed. He wondered how their stories would compare with those concocted by people who were definitely known not to have had any such experience.

Sixteen volunteers, "who knew little of and cared less about UFOs", were enlisted. Each "witness" was hypnotised and given the suggestion that they had been involved in a UFO-abduction situation. The subject was taken, step by step, through a stereotype abduction sequence, with only the bare bones of each phase being supplied:

1. Subject perceives a UFO.
2. Subject is taken aboard.
3. Subject perceives the interior of the UFO.
4. Subject perceives occupants.
5. Subject is "examined" by them.
6. Subject is given a "message".
7. Subject is returned.
8. Aftermath, involving possible behavioural effects.

At each stage, the subject was asked to describe what s/he perceived. What the investigators expected was:

that we would get garbage from the imaginary subjects – an amalgam of TV, film, sci/fi and UFO lore from media and myth. We presumed we would thus have a means of determining "real" accounts

from phony ones. No wonder we were stunned when both our first two subjects (and most of the rest) just had verbal diarrhoea all over that hospital room. Because that means that there was no difference between real and imaginary close encounters, and thus no real abductions. Ultimately it was all in the mind.

To get the full impact, the accounts have to be studied in detail. These sample extracts tell how subjects, during the second phase, perceived being taken aboard the alien spacecraft:

- "A long tube came out of it, and it was about 0.75 metre (2 ft) above me ... and this long cylinder-like tube came down. It was grey and ... was like all coloured lights inside of it ... I seemed to be floating for a second, and then I was inside"
- "...gentle suction ... it just sort of drew me up into it, sort of through the bottom ... like some sort of tunnel of air and light, drawing me up inside of it ... I'm inside of a tube when I first come in ..."
- "I was pulled in ... a particle of dust into a vacuum cleaner. I mean, I'm just suddenly there ..."

These quotations are from the fantasies of the *imaginary* abductees, yet they match closely accounts given time and again by "real" abductees. The experience almost invariably starts with very bright lights, often pulsating. The witness experiences a sense of "floating" when being taken from one location to another, often passing through solid walls or floors, and has a feeling of "paralysis" at various moments. The witness is taken into a big, brightly lit room and sees "TV screens" aboard the spacecraft on which scenes are presented by the abductors. The UFO becomes larger and smaller ... and so on. Yet these complex stories have been replicated in the minds of people with minimal interest in the subject, and with no conscious awareness of having read abduction accounts – certainly not with sufficient attention to have noted such detail.

Informal experiments by independent researcher Dennis Stillings confirm the Lawson/McCall findings. The original

stimulus with data from the imagination, memory, or knowledge about UFOs to create an encounter experience so intense that it is perceived as physically real.

However, though their "stories" are similar, there is a marked difference in the way the "real" and the "imaginary" abductees respond emotionally to their experience. This is not surprising. Lawson's subjects were volunteers, and even under hypnosis would be subconsciously aware of that fact. They were not subject to the stress and other psychological factors that affect the "real" abductees. Consequently, we would not expect them to suffer the psychological after-effects experienced

...but their creations have no firmer basis in reality than the science-fiction scenarios of H G Wells or the "pulp" writers of the 1920s and 1930s ...

Cinema and television producers have no difficulty creating scenes which echo the abductees' stories ...

small-scale study would need to be more solidly grounded however, and the protocol modified to take in other parameters, before any conclusive inferences could be justified.

Nevertheless the central finding is unequivocal – such similarities cannot be explained away as coincidence or cryptomnesia (thoughts that are really memories). It is simply unrealistic to suppose that each and every one of the volunteers was drawing on hidden memories of abduction stories they had forgotten they'd read, or even experienced themselves!

Lawson and McCall suggest that what may be happening in a "real" abduction experience is that the witness, triggered by some external stimulus such as a bright pulsating light, combines the

by the "real" abductees – amnesia, dreams, nightmares or psychic experiences, and a variety of physical effects ranging from nausea and migraine to scars and scratches which may or may not be stigmatic.

The abductionists often point to these behavioural features and physical stigmata as evidence for the reality of the abduction experience. But while they certainly show that an experience of *some kind* has occurred, they do not prove that the individual was abducted by aliens. All they demonstrate is that the "real" abductee is in a truly emotional state – but it is at least as likely that a witness has an abduction experience because he is in an emotional state as that his emotional state is the consequence of an abduction experience.

... and ultimately they tell us more about the inner world of our hopes and fears than about anything occurring in the real world.

VISIONS OF THE VIRGIN MARY

The issues are probably seen at their clearest in one of the most striking forms of visitation by otherworldly beings – encounters with Mary, the mother of Jesus of Nazareth, who is supposed by many to return to Earth in her own physical likeness.

The Roman Catholic Church believes, on minimal authority, that Mary was a specially privileged person, who though she may have started her adult life as a Palestinian housewife, ended it in some transcended form due to having been chosen to carry and bring into the world the "son of God" – that is to say, God made flesh. Catholic teaching says that when Mary died she was "taken to Heaven", and exists now on some superhuman level. However, she still retains many of her human attributes, in particular a concern for suffering humanity. For this reason she makes periodic visits to Earth.

Several thousand claims to have encountered her during these visits have been recorded, most of them either by Catholic believers or by persons wavering over whether to believe. Not all of these have received the approval of the Church authorities, though a good many have. But many questions impose themselves.

What is seen when the Virgin is seen? Surely it is not her physical body, the one she had when she lived on Earth, miraculously preserved? Apart from anything else, almost everyone who sees her describes her differently.

Since it doesn't make sense that she would herself vary her appearance for each visit, we must suppose that it is the visionary herself who is responsible for the variations. Does this mean that visions of Mary are nothing but hallucinations, possessing no objective basis? Not necessarily: some kind of interaction between Mary and the mind of the visionaries could be involved. Perhaps they see her as they expect to see her, consciously or unconsciously.

I have been privileged to personally know a girl who met the Virgin Mary on many occasions. In October 1981, Blandine Piegay of La Talaudière, near Lyon in south-west France, was told by an angel as she walked to school that she would shortly meet the Virgin Mary. A few days later she did so – the first of more than thirty meetings during which she talked with Mary in the kitchen of the family home. The Virgin gave Blandine advice about her own life, urged her father not to drink so much, told Blandine she should not eat so many sweets … and passed on the customary warnings for mankind, that

The Virgin Mary with the Baby Jesus in arms appears before the adoring crowds.

we should mend our wicked ways.

No one else saw Mary. There is no material evidence of the visits. Though thousands came by car and coach to visit the humble house which the Queen of Heaven had deigned to visit, the local curé was skeptical and advised people to stay away. The Catholic Church has never recognized Blandine's experiences as genuine. Yet she herself continues to insist that the meetings really took place.

About a hundred years earlier, another French teenager had eleven visions of the Virgin Mary. But few of the millions of pilgrims who flock to Lourdes every year are aware that Bernadette Soubirous was by no means the first person in the district to report a meeting with the Virgin Mary, nor that she was only one of dozens of people – mostly adolescents like herself – who had visionary experiences at Lourdes about the same time. Confronted with this disconcerting situation, even that perceptive researcher, the Jesuit Herbert Thurston, has to temporize. Thurston accepts Bernadette's visions as genuine and the rest as spurious, but the criteria by which he makes the distinction are not precise. His decision, like the Church's decision not to believe Blandine, seems rather arbitrary.

Should the rest of us believe that fourteen-year old Blandine had an otherworldly visitation? That *something* happened to her seems certain. But that the mother of Jesus – even if she is surviving in some form elsewhere in the Cosmos – is revisiting Earth in order to talk with a French teenager is so implausible that it seems sensible to look for alternative explanations.

GLENDA AND THE SPACEWOMAN

In the 1980s, I was involved in the investigation of a case involving a teenaged girl who had experienced a number of strange happenings. One day when she was twelve years old, Glenda came home from school and went upstairs to her room in the Dagenham council house where she lived with her parents and sister. A little while later she realized she was not alone in her room. With her was a stranger, female, whom she would later describe as a "spacewoman". Humanoid, but extravagantly dressed, Glenda described her as something you might see on television.

This being manifested intermittently in Glenda's life over the next five years – sometimes visibly, but generally as an unseen "presence", sensed but not seen. Sometimes she would figure in Glenda's dreams. She was neither malevolent, nor particularly benevolent, but she seemed clearly concerned for Glenda's well-being, giving her advice about her private affairs.

If she was an alien, she made no attempt to abduct Glenda onto her spaceship. If she was a demon, she made no attempt to seduce Glenda into any form of evil. If there is any being we have come across in these pages to which it is possible to compare her, it is the Guardian Angel. Of all those we have met, this type – so long as we forget the stereotype angel and picture some benevolent, caring, protective being – seems the most positive and purposeful.

But the Guardian Angel shares, with other entities, an elusive, subjective quality – it is almost invariably seen by one person and one alone. No other member of Glenda's family ever saw her "spacewoman", just as no other member of Blandine's family ever saw the Virgin Mary.

WHO BENEFITS FROM THE ENCOUNTER?

The cases of Blandine and Glenda have one thing in common, but from the point of view of this study, it is a very important thing. Both these two girls benefited personally from the experience. Blandine was given a boost in her self-esteem, while Glenda found someone to share her problems with.

The psychological well-being of two adolescent girls on planet Earth doesn't seem as though it would be a matter of concern for those who control the Universe, despite sentimental perceptions of gods who care even about the fall of a sparrow. It seems scarcely enough to justify a cosmic journey by an ascended divinity or a spaceperson. But the visits mattered very much to the two individuals concerned. So it is reasonable to ask whether they had these experiences because *they needed to have them?*

Looking back through this book, we realize that we could ask the same question concerning many, perhaps most of the cases reported. The benefits of the visitation to the visitors are generally far from evident. We have seen how the extraterrestrials take no interest in our achievements or sights, they don't rob us of our minerals or anything else, and their medical research (if that's what it is) is a farce. In his thoughtful and seductive 1998 book *The Threat*, Professor Jacobs outlines an alien agenda which seems purposeful and beneficial, to them if not to us. There is no objective source for this agenda however; he has pieced it together, item by item, from hints derived from the stories told by the abductees themselves. He asserts that "the evidence suggests that all the alien procedures serve a reproductive agenda", but that "evidence" could as well be an artifact of the mind-set of the abductees as an indication of alien intention.

On the other hand, time after time, the encounter seems to do a great job for the individual experiencer, whether Moses on Sinai, Star People or visionaries of the Virgin. Could it be that this is the *primary* purpose of the event, not merely a secondary side-effect?

An important clue is one thread which runs through a wide range of the experiences of contactees and abductees. They are changed by their experience, and frequently, the witness claims after-effects which are distinctly *positive.*

Here is a witness from the Laramie Rocky Mountain conferences:

> Because of my encounter in June 1977, I became more sensitive to the true meaning and the realistic value of life itself! On a spiritual level, it awakened a dormant knowledge ... My "Cosmic Companions" have given me the

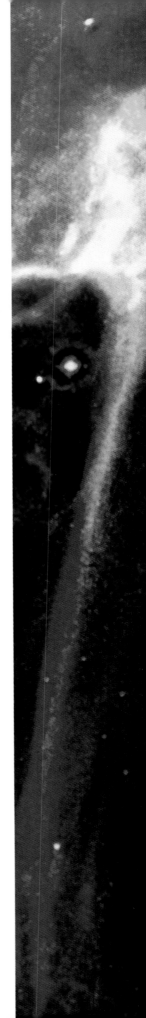

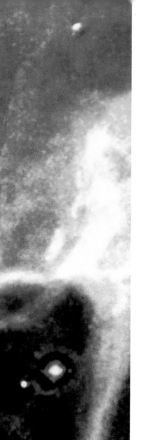

opportunity to grow spiritually and spiral upwards.

Folklorist Peter Rojcewicz says that the lives of witnesses are frequently changed by their experience. "Some become more successful in their jobs and marriages and report a joy of life" Scores of abductees have testified to what amounts to a "born again" experience as a result of their encounter with extraterrestrials, yet all that ostensibly happened to them was they received a cold, dispassionate medical inspection from unfeeling aliens who didn't give a damn about their human guinea pigs and seemingly had no other object than to acquire biological information about the human species.

It is hard to make sense of this seeming contradiction other than by supposing that the ostensible abduction and examination constitutes only an objective cover-story masking a

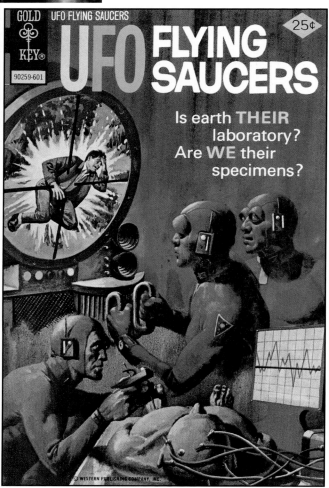

Fantasy writers have perceived aliens as conducting heartless experiments on humankind: do abduction stories, too, originate in the imagination?

subjective experience. We may go further. We may suppose that the inner, subjective story may actually be more important than the outer, objective one. In fact, we may even go further still – we may consider the possibility that the outer, ostensible, objective story has no importance or reality at all, but is simply a device, an elaborately constructed decor to provide a stage for what is *really* important, the subjective experience which the individual undergoes.

NEGATIVE CONSEQUENCES OF BELIEF

It can be argued that, since these experiences are beneficial, it doesn't much matter whether they are "real" or not. Whether beings visit us from a physical other world, from other levels of reality, or from the depths of the subconscious mind, is unimportant – it is the effects which are significant.

That point of view might be acceptable if the effects were *always* beneficial. Unfortunately that isn't the case. Beliefs can lead to actions whose consequences are disastrous. Think of the followers of Marshall Applewhite who in 1997 convinced that they were going to be transported to a great extraterrestrial spaceship travelling in the wake of the Hale-Bopp comet, killed themselves. It is not an isolated example.

Gloria Lee Byrd was an American contactee, author of two books detailing her connections with the extraterrestrials, and founder of the "Cosmon Research Foundation", which had 2000 members. In the autumn of 1962 – at which time she was thirty-seven years old – together with a follower, Hedy Hood, she went to Washington with plans for a spaceship channelled from her Space Contact, "J.W." from the planet Jupiter. They had intended to stay only two days, but when government officials refused to look at the plans, they booked into a Washington hotel where she announced that "J.W. has ordered me to go on a

fast for peace until he sends a "light elevator" to take me to Jupiter". Gloria began her fast on September 23. Her husband learned that she was ill and sent an ambulance to the hotel on November 28, but four days later she died in hospital. Her companion was indignant with the police for taking Gloria away, accusing them of "ruining a scientific experiment for peace".

"Woman dies after 4-week wait for UFO" was the headline of the Duluth *News-Tribune & Herald* on November 18, 1982. The report told how a motorist found thirty-eight year old Gerald Flach semiconscious on a remote trail. He said his friend needed medical attention, but when the rescue squad found his companion – forty-eight-year old Laverne Landis – in their car, she was dead of hypothermia, dehydration and starvation. The car was parked in a side road, snowed in and out of fuel.

At the bidding of "messages" received by Laverne, the couple had driven to Loon Lake, at the end of Gunflint Trail, close to Lake Superior near the Canadian border. There – living on the front seat of their compact car, drinking water from the lake and scarcely eating – they had waited for more than four weeks in the expectation of meeting extraterrestrials who never came.

In March 1993, at Wellington, New Zealand, twenty-five year old Wallace Waru Iopata and forty-five-year old Huia Tawhai, two followers of the Indian guru Sai Baba, felt called on to spiritually "cleanse" the latter's husband, seventy-nine year old Erueti Tawhai. After rituals including having sex beside him, they castrated him with a butcher's knife and cut off his penis, but unfortunately he died as a result. His companions dismembered his body and tried to burn it, but the house caught fire. Firemen who came to the scene found the two survivors standing naked outside the house – they explained that a UFO was coming to take them to Australia.

In June 1986, police at Harlesden in north-west London, received a phone call from a woman who said that she and her grand-daughters had been attacked by burglars. She met them at the door in a blood-stained nightie and showed them the lifeless bodies of the children, but police quickly realized her story was false.

As a result of her UFO beliefs, fifty-seven year old Gloria Stephens believed she was visited regularly by aliens who beamed her aboard their spaceship. She kept plastic bags full of clothing and belongings against the day when they took her away for good. Among many bizarre beliefs, she came to believe that her grandchildren, ten-year old Tasha and seven-year old Andrea, were in danger from the aliens. A machine like a giant vacuum cleaner would suck them to another planet. To save them from the spacemen, she decided to kill them. When they came on a holiday visit, she knifed them and herself, taking an overdose of drugs for good measure, expecting to be reunited with her granddaughters in Paradise. When she did not die, she called the police. Found guilty of manslaughter, she was placed in a psychiatric hospital.

Events such as these show that it *is* important to know what is really happening when an individual claims to be in contact with beings from other worlds. It is not a question of asking whether we should or shouldn't believe Jeanne d'Arc when she tells us she has spoken with angels and they have instructed her to take up arms against the English, or Travis Walton when he tells us he was abducted by extraterrestrials, or Moses when he comes down from Mount Sinai with the Tables of the Law. They, like Blandine and Glenda, may well be telling the truth as they see it. It is even possible they are telling the truth as the rest of us would see it.

So it is not a question of *denying* the experience, or necessarily of questioning its value. But we need to *understand* their encounters before we can know what response to make. That involves deciding whether or not these encounters involve beings from other worlds.

OPERATORS AND THINGS

Of all the claims of encounters with beings from other worlds, there is probably none which better helps us to understand the nature of the experience than Barbara O'Brien's 1958 account of her experiences with otherworldly "operators".

What happened was that, following personal troubles involving a lifestyle conflict, O'Brien had an encounter with some otherworldly entities who she called "operators". They persuaded her to pack her bags and leave home, family, job, everything. For months they kept her wandering around the United States, taking casual jobs and living as best she could. All this time, she was living on two worlds – that of the real world, work and the rest, and that of her "operators". Apart from occasional breakdowns, she managed the balancing act pretty well, though she was not helped when she consulted a psychiatrist who decided the best place for her was a mental clinic.

Finally the day came when she said to herself that enough was enough, confronted her situation, and rounded on the beings, telling them to get the hell out of her life. Only then did she realize that had been the purpose of the experience, to get her to take charge of her own destiny.

What makes her account so valuable is that she is an intelligent, thoughtful and perceptive person who is able to examine her own situation lucidly and objectively. She realizes that what happened to her was that her subconscious mind created a "psychodrama" for her, enabling her to act out her own situation as though it were a stage play:

> There is an amazing lack of accurate knowledge among laymen concerning the effects of schizophrenia. The most prevalent notion is that the individual becomes two people, two distinct personalities, or even multiple personalities ... In most cases, however, the unconscious appears to prefer not the techniques of the actor, but those of the director. It does not create a new personality, but, instead, stages a play. The major difference is that the conscious mind is permitted to remain, an audience of one, watching a drama on which it cannot walk out ... As you sit watching your Martian, it is your unconscious mind which is flashing the picture before your eyes, sounding the man's voice in your ears. More than this, it is blowing a fog of

Barbara O'Brien came to realize that the otherworldly "operators" who had taken control of her life were creations of her own subconscious mind.

hypnosis over your conscious mind so that consciously you see and hear, and the delusions that accompany the hallucinations are real.

THE ULTIMATE QUESTION

If our Earth is receiving otherworldly visitors, why don't more of us get to meet them? With that question comes another, too: Are the people who do meet them lucky, unlucky, special – or simply deluded?

In every case cited in this book, there were people – sometimes only the witness, sometimes many others – who believed that an actual encounter took place with visitors from other worlds. It is equally true to say that, regarding each and every case, there

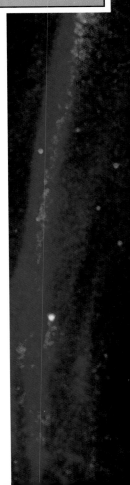

were people who listened to the same story and either rejected it out of hand, or found some alternative explanation for it which did not involve otherworldly beings.

Though these visitors have been reported as coming to our planet throughout more than 2000 years of history – and possibly for long before that – there is not a scrap of totally convincing evidence that they have actually done so. Subjective human testimony abounds, most of it from sincere people who deserve to be listened to with respect, but it is not supported by any objective evidence.

On the other hand, those who offer explanations which do not involve otherworldly beings – such as psychological experiences of some kind – are also unable to provide evidence for their version of the matter. Apart from the general difficulty of proving a negative, we have seen that there are some cases in which, if they really happened as narrated, we must invoke either otherworldly beings or paranormal powers of some nature. For example, there are many documented cases in which information is provided which the witness would not normally have access to, and which often results in someone averting a disaster because of this information.

What should our attitude be towards the story-tellers we have met in this book, or towards someone who comes to us with their own story of

Unexplained magic and power: an extraterrestrial spacecraft hovers over the ancient, stone worship sites of the druids and witches.

otherworldly visitors?

Certainly, we must not look for a single all-or-nothing explanation. Probably no one believes in the physical reality of every single one of the otherworldly visitations we have looked at. But if we cannot accept them all, which of them, if any, should we accept and which reject? In the end, each of us must judge each instance on its own merits, and come to a personal decision.

I deliberately saved Barbara O'Brien's experience with beings from other worlds till the last, because I believe it is her case more than any other which shows us how to see through the outer facade to the inner reality of the otherworldly encounter. Her final evaluation of what happened to her is that the experience – traumatic and frequently frightening though it may have been – was not a breakdown, a negative experience, but a necessary, purposeful and ultimately beneficial process, a process which restored order and balance to her life.

The same may be true of many, perhaps most, ostensible otherworldly encounters. Glenda's spacewoman, Blandine's Virgin, Andreasson's aliens – all may be the equivalent of guardian angels whose function is to set the individual on a surer, better course of life. Seen in this light, even seemingly horrific encounters – alien attacks, demonic possession, and so on – can be seen as ultimately beneficial, a kind of spiritual surgery.

Sometimes the experience turns out badly, just as surgery sometimes fails. Gloria Lee Byrd, Laverne Landis, and Andrea, Tasha and even Gloria Stephens were victims, due to lack of understanding. But with rare exceptions, throughout all the myths, legends, claimed experiences and case histories we have looked at in this book, there runs one constant and very revealing thread. The ones who benefit most from these visitations are not the visiting aliens, but we on Earth who receive their visits. They don't need us – it is we who need these visitors from other worlds.

Science has put man on the Moon and given us this view of Earth from there. However the extent of Space and who or what inhabit it is still unknown.

INDEX

Picture Credits

The publishers would like to thank the following sources for their kind permission to reproduce the pictures in this book:

Corbis/Everett/*Contact* WarnerSouth Side Amusement 1997, *The X-Files, Close Encounters of the Third Kind*, Columbia/EMI 1977, Araldo de Luca, Roger Rossmeyer/Science Photo Library; Mary Evans Picture Library/Michael Buhler; Fortean Picture Library/Lisa Anders; The Image Bank; Science Photo Library/BSIP/Krassovsky, Julian Baum, Victor Habbick Visions, David Hardy, Roger Harris, Erich Schremp; David Tarn

Every effort has been made to acknowledge correctly and contact the source and/or copyright holder of each picture, and Carlton Books Limited apologizes for any unintentional errors or omissions which will be corrected in future editions of this book.

About the Author

Hilary Evans is an acknowledged authority on UFOs, extra-terrestrial experiences and the paranormal. He writes and lectures on anomaly research, psychical research, folklore and myth, and related subjects. He is a member of the Society for Psychical Research, the American Society for Psychical Research; the Society for Scientific Exploration; the Association for the Scientific Study of Anomalous Phenomena and the Folklore Society. He has written books on many aspects of anomaly research, notably *Intrusions*; *Visions, Apparitions and Alien Visitors*; *Gods, Spirits, and Cosmic Guardians*; *Frontiers of Reality*; and *Alternate States of Consciousness*. He is the author of four books on UFOs: *UFOs, the Greatest Mystery*; *The Evidence for UFOs*; *UFOs 1947–1987* and *UFOs 1947–1997* and has published many articles on these subjects. He was also writer–consultant for *Almanac of the Uncanny* and several other Reader's Digest publications. He lives in London.